Law for

Laymen

AN AUSTRALIAN BOOK OF
LEGAL ADVICE AND INFORMATION.
CLEAR, CONCISE & PRACTICAL.

BY

C. H. CHOMLEY

Barrister-at-Law.

REVISED AND BROUGHT UP TO DATE.

Biography of C. H. Chomley

Charles Henry Chomley was born on 28th April 1868 in Sale, Victoria, Australia. He was the son of banker, Henry Baker Chomley and his wife Eliza (daughter of lawyer and politician, Thomas Turner à Beckett). The second of four children, Chomley attended Trinity College, University of Melbourne, graduating with a BA in 1888, and an LL.B in 1889, consequently being accepted to the Victorian Bar in 1891. Chomley left the legal profession two years later however, and established a farming partnership in Australia with his cousin, Frank Chomley. With a group of friends, he settled in the King River Valley in northeast Victoria.

Chomley returned to Melbourne due to heart problems in 1900 - a move which signalled the launch of his journalistic career. Here, he took up editorship of the illustrated weekly *Arena*. Dedicated to the arts, politics, and society gossip, the magazine also demonstrated strong support of both the suffragette movement and free trade. Over the following few years, Chomley wrote and co-wrote several works, before setting sail for London in 1907. In 1908 he became editor of the *British Australasian*, a weekly tabloid that provided Antipodeans in London a link to news, markets, weather, and society information from home. Under Chomley's editorship, the magazine developed a distinctly more artistic tone, with some summer numbers featuring sketches, poetry, short stories and interviews with prominent members of the Australasian arts community in London. He remained editor of the paper until his death in 1942.

Chomley was heavily interested in both Australian and British politics, and published his novel, *Mark Meredith: A Tale of Socialism* in 1905. It is an important work in the Australian literary canon as it provides not only an insight into the political sphere, but also the emotions of the Australian people at this changeable time. It depicts a fictitious period in Australian history where socialism has been in place for numerous years, according to Chomley, an entirely negative development. Another politically inspired work is *Protection in Canada and Australasia* (1904), discussing the federations of the British Empire in relation to free trade and protectionist battles. He maintained his early interest in the law though and wrote *The True Story of the Kelly Gang of Bushrangers* (1900), a highly researched biography utilising court documents, police records and court evidence. This was followed by *The Wisdom of Esau* in 1901, another fictional work examining land laws within Australia.

Chomley died on 21st October 1942, in London, England, aged seventy four.

PREFACE.

THIS little book, in which I have had the assistance
of a member of the Victorian Bar, who does not wish
his name mentioned, is, as the title states, intended
only for laymen. There are lawyers, indeed, who may
sometimes find it useful to refresh their memories, but
its aim is to give, in handy form, and with a generality
of statement to which the expert might take exception,
some of the most important principles of the common
law, and certain statutory provisions concerning a
number of affairs of business and every-day life.
Portions of the book deal with special Victorian legislation, such as the Companies Acts; but the great
bulk of the information given concerns the law which
is common to all the States of Australia and to England. Where not otherwise specified, any Acts of Parliament quoted are those of Victoria. In such cases,
with rare exceptions, legislation of a similar nature,
varying in more or less important detail, is in force
in other parts of the Commonwealth. It is not
claimed that a layman will be wise to rely upon the
guidance of this volume in disputed legal matters.
A layman, indeed, is ill-advised if he rules his conduct
on such matters upon anything he reads. Simple
books upon a subject so vast and complex as law
are necessarily simple at the expense of exhaustive-
ness, and the huge text books and lengthy reports

which supplement the practising lawyer's professional experience are bewildering and misleading to
anyone but an expert. In serious matters, therefore, the author has merely endeavoured to tell, in
a manner intelligible to anybody, " what to do until
the lawyer comes." If he has succeeded in this, he
believes the book, full of imperfections as he knows
it to be, will be useful to thousands of men and
women in giving them some definite knowledge of
their legal rights and duties, and the rights and duties
of those with whom they enter into legal relations,
intentionally or unintentionally, in the course of their
daily affairs.

INDEX.

LAW FOR LAYMEN.

AGENT AND PRINCIPAL.

Where one person authorises another to represent him, or act on his behalf, and undertakes to be answerable for what that other does within the scope of the authority conferred on him, and such other person undertakes to accept the authority, and obey all lawful instructions which the first person gives him with regard to it, the first-mentioned person is called a principal, the second an agent, and the relation of agency is created between them.

Where the agent acts and contracts in the name of the principal, the principal alone is responsible to third parties, and he alone can sue them on agreements made on his behalf by his agent. In other cases the agent may pledge his own credit as well as that of his principal, in which case a third party may hold either of them responsible, and is himself responsible to either of them.

A principal is always bound to indemnify the agent for all expenses and losses and liabilities incurred by the latter in the proper execution of his authority, and the agent is bound to account to the principal for all profits acquired through the agency.

An agent who commits a wrong with the authority of his principal is liable, as well as the principal, in spite of that authority, and he has no claim against the principal for indemnity for the consequences of doing a wrongful act. These remarks apply to private agents, and not to agents of the Crown or Government.

An agent appointed to sign a deed must be appointed by a deed called a " Power of Attorney." An agent appointed to sell land should be appointed in writing, otherwise the contract will not bind the seller.

WHAT MAY BE DONE THROUGH AN AGENT—As a general rule a man may do by an agent anything he may do himself; but he may not engage an agent to exercise powers, authorities, and duties of a confidential or personal nature conferred upon himself, or which involve the exercise of his personal discretion. Thus an agent must not, as a rule, delegate his authority to another agent, since he is chosen for his personal fitness to exercise it.

Where two or more agents are given joint authority, they can only validly execute it by acting in concert, unless otherwise provided.

Agency may be implied from the conduct or situation of the parties. The auctioneer at a sale by auction is an implied agent for the purpose of signing the contract of sale on behalf of the highest bidder. To a certain extent a wife has implied authority to pledge her husband's credit, as for necessaries, and the same rule applies to a woman living with a man as his wife.

Where one person does an act on behalf of another without precedent authority, the other may make himself a principal, and the first person his agent, by express or implied ratification of the act.

If a person so acts as to lead others to believe that a second person is his agent, he will not be permitted to deny the agency to the loss of a third person who acted on the faith of its existence.

EXTENT OF AGENT'S AUTHORITY—When an agent is authorised to receive payment of money, he has, prima facie, only authority to receive payment in the ordinary course of business, and in cash. Thus, an auctioneer has no authority to take a bill of exchange or promissory note in payment. The taking of cheques and giving of credit may be authorised as being part of the ordinary course of the business in which the agent is acting; but the general rule is that an agent to receive payment is authorised only to take cash.

Subject to express instructions from the principal, an agent has implied authority to do everything necessary to effectively carry out his agency. Thus, authority to find a purchaser for a property implies authority to state facts bearing on its value; authority to sell a horse implies authority to warrant it, if either principal or agent is a horse dealer, or a person accustomed to buying and selling horses; a bailiff authorised to levy a distress has implied authority to receive the rent and expenses due; a manager of an estate has implied authority to grant the usual and customary leases; a traveller for the sale of goods has implied authority to receive payment of the price of goods sold.

DUTIES OF AN AGENT—The degree of skill, care, and diligence required of an agent depend on whether he is acting gratuitously or for payment, and on the nature of the agency.

An agent who acts gratuitously is bound to conduct a principal's business with such knowledge, skill, and care as he habitually exercises with regard to his own; but he is not liable for want of skill unless he holds himself out as possessing it, or unless he acts in a manner so unskilful as to be unreasonable in a person in his situation.

An agent acting for reward is bound to exercise such a degree of skill, care, and diligence as is usual in the business in which he is employed and necessary for the proper performance of his duties. What is reasonable and usual care, etc., is in each case a question of fact. It is the duty of a patent agent to know the law relating to the practice of obtaining patents, and of an insurance broker to know what provisions are usually inserted in policies which he undertakes to effect.

It is the duty of an agent to act with perfect good faith towards his principal; and if an agent employed to purchase property purchases it on his own behalf, and it is made over to him, he becomes a trustee thereof for his principal. If he has any personal interest in a sale or purchase negotiated by him, he must disclose the fact to his principal. If an agent for the sale of property purchase it himself without informing his principal, the principal, on discovering the fact, may either repudiate the transaction or may affirm it, and recover from the agent any profit the agent has made.

Whenever an agent, in the course, or by means of the agency, acquires any benefit or profit without the consent of the principal, it is deemed to be received on the principal's behalf, and the value or amount of it must be accounted for and paid over to him.

LIABILITY OF AGENT TO HIS PRINCIPAL —An agent is liable to his principal to make good any loss arising from the agent's negligence or other breach of duty, provided it is a loss that might be reasonably expected to result therefrom. For instance, an agent is liable for loss occasioned by neglect of instructions to insure, and for parting with goods without payment in defiance of instructions. He is not liable for loss when he strictly follows instructions, even though they be imprudent, nor where he has exercised his best judgment in a matter of discretion.

AGENT'S REMUNERATION—The remuneration of an agent, either by commission or otherwise, is settled either by arrangement or by the custom or usage prevailing in the business in which he acts. If it is provided that an agent shall receive commission after a certain event has happened, as after the payment of the purchase money for a property which the agent is endeavouring to sell has been paid, he cannot claim commission before that time, even though the principal's default prevent the sale; but the agent may sue the principal for damages for wrongfully preventing him from earning his commission.

If the commission is payable on the agent doing something, it is payable when he has done his part. For instance, when an agent is promised commission for securing a loan, he is entitled to be paid when he has introduced to his principal a man able and willing to lend the money on the specified terms even though the principal do not borrow it. Similarly, commission promised on goods bought through an agent is payable when the agent has obtained the orders, although the principal does not execute them.

It must be remembered, however, that a principal has the right, in the absence of agreement to the contrary, to revoke the authority of the agent at any time before it is completely exercised, and it will then depend on circumstances whether the agent is entitled to remuneration for the work he has already done. An agent is entitled to no payment in respect of any transaction which he knows to be illegal, nor of any transaction in which his negligence has prevented the principal from reaping any benefit.

PRINCIPAL'S RESPONSIBILITY TO THIRD PARTIES ON CONTRACTS—The principal is generally bound by the acts of his agent to any person who knows that the agent is such, and has no reason to suppose that he is exceeding his authority when he is apparently acting within it.

Where the agent's act is not within the usual scope of the authority of such an agent, the principal is not bound by it, unless the agent was, in fact, authorised. The admission of an agent is evidence against his principal if it is made in the ordinary course of the agent's employment, and relates to a matter on which he was employed when he made the statement. For instance, when there was a question whether a parcel had been stolen from a railway, the statement of a station-master to a constable as to the absconding of a porter was admitted as evidence against the company. If an agent is employed to pay workmen, his promise to pay is admission which can be used against the principal that the money is due. But an agent's statement is not evidence against the principal unless it is made in the ordinary course of his employment.

Notice to the agent is, as a general rule, notice to the principal, and a principal is deemed to have notice of facts which the agent learns in the course of his employment if they are of such a kind as it is the agent's duty to communicate to his principal. This rule does not apply where the agent is engaged in a fraud against his principal, which prevents the agent disclosing the facts.

A contract made by an agent, as a rule, binds his principal, except in the case of contracts by deed, bills of exchange, promissory notes, and cheques. These latter, which are promises to pay in various forms, may in certain cases be binding only on those actually signing them.

Where a person deals with an agent, not knowing him to be so, and afterwards discovers that he has a principal, such person may sue either the principal or the agent. But if a person knowingly deals with an agent, and chooses to give credit to the agent exclusively, he cannot afterwards turn round and sue the principal.

Where the principal may be sued on his agent's contract, he may also sue on it.

PRINCIPAL'S LIABILITY FOR AGENT'S WRONGS—A principal is liable civilly to third persons for the negligence or other wrongs of an agent, provided the agent was acting either expressly under authority or in the ordinary course of his employment. In the latter case, the fact that the principal has expressly ordered the agent not to do the act complained of is no defence.

Thus a principal is liable if his agent, in the ordinary course of employment, commits a trespass, or negligently injures a person by careless driving. If, however, the agent, though using the principal's horse and vehicle, were doing so for private ends, and not in the course of his employment, the principal would not be liable. Nor was the principal held liable when his agent, a bailiff, committed an unnecessary and unauthorised assault while levying a distress. To do this was outside the scope of his employment.

LIABILITY OF AGENT TO THIRD PARTIES —An agent is not liable on a contract made by him purely and avowedly in his representative capacity. In written contracts, to escape liability he should distinctly describe himself as an agent. In the case of a deed, the principal, and not the agent, should be named as a party, as otherwise the agent may be liable, even though he be described as executing the deed on behalf of a principal named therein.

Where an agent wrongfully professes to contract on behalf of another—when he has, in fact, no authority to do so—he may be held liable for any damages suffered by the person who contracts with him, through such person acting on the belief that the agent was authorised to bind his principal.

Agents, as a rule, have no right to sue personally on contracts made in their representative capacity. An auctioneer, however, may sue for the price of goods, because he has a special property in them, and may have a lien on them for his fees.

THE END OF AN AGENCY—The authority of an agent is ended—

By the expiration of the time, if any, for which it was given.

By the loss or destruction of the subject matter of the agency.

By the happening of any event rendering the continuance of the agency unlawful.

By the complete performance of the contract of agency.

By the death, lunacy, or (in some cases) the insolvency of principal or agent, or by either giving the other notice (in revocable agencies) of the withdrawal of his assent to the agency continuing.

AUCTIONEERS.

Any person who acts as an auctioneer without having obtained a licence is liable for each offence to a penalty not exceeding two hundred pounds, and is incapacitated from holding a licence for three years.

TWO DESCRIPTIONS OF LICENCES—There are two descriptions of licence, a "general auctioneer's licence" and a "district auctioneer's licence," for each of which a fee of twenty-five pounds is payable. A general auctioneer's licence authorises the holder to follow the occupation of an auctioneer in any part of Victoria. A district auctioneer's licence authorises the holder to follow the occupation within the police district in which application for the same has been made. No district auctioneer's licence applies to the cities of Melbourne or Geelong. No auctioneer under a general licence may follow his occupation in any other police district than Melbourne or Geelong until he has registered his name, place of residence, and the particulars of his licence in the court of petty sessions of the district where he proposes to do so, nor until a certificate of such registration has been indorsed on the licence by the chairman of the court.

Any person desirous of obtaining an auctioneer's licence for any year must deliver to the clerk of the court of petty sessions for the district a notice in writing in the form in the second schedule of the *Auction Sales Act 1890*, together with a certificate of character signed by six respectable householders resident in the district. The clerk then posts in the court house a list of applicants fourteen days at least before the applications are disposed of by the court of petty sessions. These provisions do not apply when the application is for a renewal of the licence. When the court deals with the application, any person is entitled to object, and the court deals with the application after hearing evidence. A renewal is issued as a matter of course, and it is not necessary for the applicant to appear, unless notice of intention to object has been sent to him by the objector, and a deposit of five pounds paid to the clerk of the court, at least eight clear days before the day on which the application is to be disposed of. Except under these conditions no objection can be made to the renewal of a licence. The court of petty sessions then hears the application, and if it does not sustain the objection may order that the whole or any part of the deposit be paid to the applicant as costs.

After dealing with the applications for licences or renewals, the court of petty sessions issue certificates and forward within fourteen days a list of the names of those to whom certificates have been granted.

The applicant must then lodge the certificate, and the sum to be paid for a licence in the office of the Treasurer of Victoria, or some other place appointed by the Governor-in-Council, before the twenty-eighth day from the date of the certificate. An extension of time for a period not exceeding six weeks may be granted by the Governor-in-Council on special application. Unless the certificate is lodged and the fee paid the certificate becomes null and void; after it has been duly lodged, a licence is issued, and a notice thereof published in the *Government Gazette*.

The fourth Tuesday in November is the day fixed for the annual meeting of justices for the licencing of auctioneers, and any two justices are sufficient to constitute such meeting. Provision is made for adjournment if two justices are not present, and at an adjourned meeting one justice may act if two justices are not present by one o'clock. Under certain conditions, in the case of emergency, a special meeting may be authorised by the Governor-in-Council.

CONDUCT OF BUSINESS—An auctioneer may not sell any article or real estate after sunset or before sunrise under a penalty of not less than five or more than fifty pounds.

Music must not be played during a sale excepting such as may be necessary for trial of an instrument about to be sold; nor may a sale be held in an unsuitable room or building; nor may the auctioneer permit any riotous or disorderly conduct in a sale room. For such offences there is a liability to a penalty not exceeding ten pounds.

Any unlicenced person pretending to be an auctioneer is liable to a penalty of not less than twenty nor more than one hundred pounds. No person holding a victualler's licence, nor his partner, is competent to hold a licence as an auctioneer. Auctioneers are required to keep a registry of cattle sold by them, and transmit a weekly return to the court of petty sessions. This is open to inspection to any police officer or justice of the peace free of cost, and to every other person on payment of a fee of two shillings and sixpence. An auctioneer before selling cattle must require from the owner or possessor a certificate of respectability from some known and respectable person. If he fail to do this he is liable to a penalty not exceeding twenty pounds; for a second offence against any of the provisions of the Act he is liable to have his licence cancelled.

The Act does not apply to certain sales by or under the authority of the Crown, or sales under order of the court, or sales of impounded animals, or goods distrained for rent, or sales under the authority of a municipal body.

An advertisement by an auctioneer that a sale will take place on a certain day does not bind the auctioneer to sell the goods, or make him liable to indemnify persons who are put to expense in order to attend the sale. Where a sale is advertised to be *without reserve*, a binding contract is created between the auctioneer and the highest bidder, who is entitled to claim the property whether the sum bid be equivalent to its value or not.

An auctioneer is an agent to sell at a public auction. Until the goods or property are sold he is the agent of the seller; immediately they are knocked down he becomes also agent of the buyer. He is deemed to be in actual possession of the goods, and he is entitled to a lien upon them for his charges. He is entitled to sue the purchaser in his own name. The authority of an auctioneer does not extend beyond the auction. His signature to the document containing the terms of sale binds both the seller and buyer; but upon a subsequent sale by private contract of unsold lots he has no authority to bind the buyer by signing. The auctioneer has a general authority to receive payment, and the principal can only receive the price from the buyer subject to his claim. Consequently, if the auctioneer sue the buyer for the price, it is no defence that the latter has paid the principal if the auctioneer's claim remain unsatisfied. But where the conditions of sale provide that a deposit only is to be paid, and the balance at a future date, the authority is only to receive the deposit. The authority of an auctioneer may be revoked at any time before the sale is effected.

Where goods are put up by auction in lots, each lot is generally the subject of a separate contract of sale, unless there is an implied agreement to the contrary. A sale is complete when the auctioneer drops the hammer, or in any other customary manner indicates that the last bid is accepted. Until this is done any bidder may retract his bid.

Where a sale by auction is not notified to be subject to a right to bid on behalf of the seller, he cannot do so; but may if such right is expressly reserved. A sale by auction may be notified to be subject to a reserved or upset price, and a right to bid at the auction may also be expressly reserved by or on behalf of the seller.

BILLS OF EXCHANGE.

A bill of exchange is an unconditional order in writing, addressed by one person to another, signed by the person giving it, requiring the person to whom it is addressed to pay on demand, or at a fixed and determinable future time, a sum certain in money to, or to the order of, a specified person or to bearer.

The law relating to bills of exchange is codified —A Commonwealth Act of Parliament, " The Bills of Exchange Act 1909"—which applies to all the Australian States. It is full of detail, and only a few general statements can be given here.

The following is an ordinary form of a bill of exchange. It must bear the proper duty stamp (in Victoria, embossed on forms printed by the Government).

£1000.

London, July 1st, 1905.

[Three] months after date [or on demand, or at sight, or on —— days after sight] pay John Jones or order one thousand pounds.

James Smith.

To William Green, Merchant, Melbourne.

THE PARTIES TO A BILL.—There must be two parties to a bill of exchange—the drawer, who gives the order to pay, and the "drawee," to whom it is given. A cheque drawn on a bank is an example of a bill of exchange in its simplest form. On bills of exchange, however, other parties commonly acquire rights and liabilities.

The drawer of a bill by drawing it engages that, on due presentment, it shall be accepted and paid according to its tenor, and that if dishonoured he will compensate the holder or any endorser who is compelled to pay it, provided that the requisite proceedings on dishonour be duly taken; is precluded from denying to a holder, in due course, the existence of the payee and his then capacity to indorse.

The person in whose favour the bill of exchange is drawn is called the "payee." On receiving the bill he may present it to the "drawee" for payment if payable on demand, and for "acceptance" if payable at some future time. Drafts, which are bills of exchange, are commonly an order to the drawee to pay the amount specified so many days "after sight." If the "drawee" accepts a bill the time begins to run after he has seen and accepted it. He then becomes the acceptor. Should the drawee refuse to accept the bill, the payee has an immediate right to sue the drawer upon it upon giving to him notice of dishonour.

Bills which order payment at some period after sight must be presented for acceptance before that time, as their being seen is a condition necessary to the running of the time, and they may be dishonoured by refusal to accept.

Should the drawee accept, the payee has a right of action, primarily against the acceptor, if the bill is not paid on its proper presentment for payment, and afterwards against the drawer who gave it to him.

The drawer has right of action against the acceptor who fails to pay.

THE HOLDERS OF A BILL,—In the course of business, bills of exchange ordinarily come into the hands of persons who were originally not parties to them. Such persons are called "holders" of the bill.

The bill may be transferred from one holder to another before it has been accepted.

A holder who takes a bill of exchange lawfully and for value, which he will be presumed to have given, thereupon acquires the right to demand payment of it from the acceptor when it becomes due—immediately if it is payable on demand—and if it is not paid by him he has a right to demand its value from the drawer on giving notice of dishonour.

INDORSEMENT—A holder of the bill may pass it on to another person. Sometimes he may do so by mere delivery. In other cases indorsement is required for the transfer, and in the latter case the holder who indorses it to another holder becomes liable to him on the bill in the event of its not being met by the acceptor. A bill may be indorsed by many different persons, and passed through many different hands, and in every case each indorser enters into certain engagements, which are as follows:—

The indorser of a bill, by indorsing it, engages that on due presentment it shall be accepted and paid according to its tenor, and that if it be dishonoured he will compensate the holder or a subsequent indorser who is compelled to pay it, provided that the requisite proceedings on dishonour be duly taken; is precluded from denying to a holder in due course the genuineness and regularity in all respects of the drawer's signature and all previous indorsements; is precluded from denying to his immediate or subsequent indorsee that the bill was, at the time of his indorsement, a valid and subsisting bill, and that he had a good title thereto.

ACCOMMODATION PARTY—A person who draws, accepts, or indorses a bill in order to oblige another person, by giving his credit and without receiving value therefor himself, is liable on the bill to a holder for value. Such a person is called an "Accommodation party." When a holder for value takes the bill, it is immaterial whether he knew any other party was an accommodation party. The mere signing of one's name without any words referring to liability constitutes indorsement, provided that, with the consent of the person so signing the bill, it goes into the hands of any other person. An indorsement may be in blank or special. In the first case, the indorser simply writes his name, and the bill then becomes payable to bearer. A special indorsement specifies the person to whom or to whose order the bill is to be payable; and in that case this person must sign before the bill can be paid or indorsed to someone else.

Where a person writes his name on the back of a cheque for which he obtains payment from some person or a bank other than that on which the cheque is drawn, he is, in fact, indorsing a bill of exchange, and incurs liability for its value to the person who holds it if it should not be paid by the bank on which it is drawn.

Speaking generally, notice in the form prescribed by the Act is required of the dishonour of a bill of exchange to all those who may have become liable on it by indorsement, before they can be called upon to pay.

VALIDITY OF A BILL—No precise form of words is essential to the validity of a bill of exchange, provided it is an unconditional order to pay as described. In Victoria, however, it must be drawn on a form with an embossed duty stamp, and no bill is good unless properly stamped.

A bill is not invalid by reason of its not being dated, or because it does not specify the place where it is payable.

Where the sum payable is expressed in words and figures, and there is a discrepancy between the two, the sum denoted by the words is the amount payable.

INLAND AND FOREIGN BILLS—Bills of exchange are of two kinds—inland bills and foreign bills. The former are those which purport on their face to be (a) both drawn and payable within Australia, Tasmania, New Zealand, or the Fiji Islands, or any Commonwealth Territory, or (b) drawn within Australia, Tasmania, New Zealand, the Fiji

Islands or any Commonwealth territory upon some person resident therein. All other bills of exchange are foreign bills. Foreign bills are greatly used in the dealings between Australian merchants and those abroad. The principles of law with regard to them are the same as those relating to inland bills, but the procedure on the dishonour of the two classes is in some respects different.   -

CHEQUES—A cheque is defined as "a bill of exchange drawn on a banker, payable on demand to or to the order of a specified person, or to bearer."

OPEN CHEQUES—An open cheque is one which, though the name of the person to whom it is payable be inserted, is not crossed, or made payable to order. It will be cashed across the counter of a bank to anyone presenting it, and, therefore, where there is possibility of a cheque being lost or getting into wrong hands, it should not be left open.

In a cheque drawn to order, the word "bearer" is struck out, and the words "or order" inserted after the name of the person to whom it is payable. The effect of this is that payment will not be made until the payee has endorsed the cheque with his signature. If he is misdescribed in the cheque, by his name being spelt wrongly, or initials being wrongly stated, he should, nevertheless, indorse the cheque with the name as used in the cheque, adding his correct signature in brackets. A cheque payable to order is quite safe from any thief before it is indorsed, unless the thief runs the risk of indorsing it with the name of the person in whose favour it is drawn. In such a case the loss would fall upon the drawer, and not upon the bank paying it in good faith in its ordinary course of business.

A cheque is crossed by drawing two lines across it, up and down. The words "& Co." are often added between the lines, but this is not necessary.

Such a cheque is crossed generally. It will not be paid across a bank counter, but must be passed through some person's account.

A cheque may be crossed specially by writing the name of some particular bank across it, in which case it must be paid into some account in that particular bank.

NOT NEGOTIABLE—If an innocent person gives value for an ordinary open or crossed cheque, he may obtain a better title to it than the person from whom he received it. That is to say, though the cheque were stolen, the innocent holder for value would be entitled to obtain the amount for which it is drawn, from the drawer. If the words "not negotiable" are written across the cheque, no person who takes it can obtain a better title than that which the person from whom he took it possessed. Therefore, the drawer who takes this precaution is safe from the danger of becoming liable to the person who inno cently gives value for a stolen cheque.

WHO MAY CROSS CHEQUES—The holder of a cheque, as well as the drawer, may cross a cheque either generally or specially, and may also add the words "not negotiable."

Only the drawer of a cheque may make it open after it has been crossed, which he does by writing the words "Pay Cash," and affixing his initials. This procedure is not sanctioned by the Act, but in practice is commonly done.

A cheque is not invalidated by being drawn on Sunday, or by being antedated. Cheques should not be postdated, since they are useless until the date which they bear arrives.

A long delay in presenting a cheque does not release the drawer of it, who remains liable for six years. He may, however, recover from the holder any damages which he suffers through unreasonable delay in presentation; and if he dies before the cheque is presented, the banker will refuse payment. In that case it can only be obtained through the executor or administrator; and since it is also possible that the funds of the drawer may become exhausted, it is well to present cheques promptly.

MISCELLANEOUS—The drawer of a cheque may " stop payment " of it by an order to his bankers, which releases them from liability to any person presenting it, but does not release the drawer from liability to anyone who innocently acquires it for value, unless it is marked " not negotiable."

Where there is a discrepancy between the words and figures in a cheque, the banker will probably not cash it without a reference to the drawer; but if the discrepancy is small, may pay the amount stated in words.

Where a cheque requires the indorsement of a person who cannot write, he should make his mark in the presence of a witness, who writes his name and address beneath it, and over it the words, " John Jones—his mark."

Where a person is too ill to write, he may put his mark to a cheque, which should be witnessed by the doctor and some other person; while the doctor should send a certificate to the bank that, though unable to write, the customer is of clear mind and understanding.

COMPANIES.

No company, association, or partnership consisting of more than ten persons, if it be for the purpose of carrying on the business of banking, or more than twenty for any other business, can be formed unless it is registered under the Companies Acts, or formed in pursuance of letters patent.

Where five or more persons are associated for any lawful purpose they may form a company with or without limited liability.

The law upon the subject is contained in the Companies Acts of Victoria, and is highly technical. There are four main divisions, comprising:—

I. Trading Companies.
II. Mining Companies.
III. Life Assurance Companies.
IV. Trustee Companies.

1. TRADING COMPANIES.—The liability of members for the debts of the company may be either

(a) UNLIMITED—In this case every member is personally liable for the company's debts, having a right of indemnity against his fellow-members. Companies with unlimited liability have, however, practically become obsolete.

(b) LIMITED BY SHARES—This is the most usual form of liability. When a company is formed, a document called the Memorandum of Association, subscribed by five or more persons, must set forth the name of the company, with the addition of the word "Limited;" the objects for which the company is formed; a declaration that the liability of the members is limited; and the amount of its registered capital, divided into shares of a certain fixed amount.

The liability of members is then limited to the
amount unpaid upon their shares; for example, if
the capital of the company consists of £10,000,
divided into 10,000 shares of £1 each, and ten shillings has been already paid upon each share, should
the company get into debt, or be wound up, each
member would be liable to pay up to the amount of
ten shillings on every share, but not more.

(c) LIMITED BY GUARANTEE—The liability
of members in a company limited by guarantee
extends to a specified amount, which each member
undertakes by the memorandum of association to
contribute to its assets in the event of its being
wound up. This style of company is confined chiefly
to associations, which do not require a capital, such
as clubs or companies which buy to re-sell.

(d) NO LIABILITY—By the acceptance of a
share in a no-liability company a person cannot be
compelled to pay any calls or contribution to the
debts of the company. If he fail to pay the call, his
shares may be forfeited; but he is under no further,
liability in respect of them. A company formed upon
this system must have the words " No Liability "
after its name. The system is that usually followed
in mining companies; it was extended to trading
companies by the *Companies Act 1896*, but has not
been adopted to any extent.

PROPRIETARY COMPANIES—A proprietary
company is one that has not more than fifty
members, and does not receive deposits, except from
its members. This form of company is, in practice,
almost exclusively confined to the conversion of a
family business or partnership into a company. It
is exempted from the necessity of complying with
many of the provisions of the Acts which apply to
other companies, such as the prohibition against
commencing business before a certain amount of
capital has been paid up, publication of balance-

sheets, and provisions as to audit. Such a company must use the word "Proprietary" after its title, before the word "Limited." Persons dealing with the company then have notice of its character, and can satisfy themselves from its registered documents as to its capital.

MEMORANDUM OF ASSOCIATION—This was described by Lord Cairns as the charter of the company. It can only be altered without the aid of the court by increasing and consolidating its capital, or converting its paid-up shares into stock. The court, if satisfied that the interests of creditors are safeguarded, may sanction alterations in the objects of the company as set forth in the memorandum of association.

ARTICLES OF ASSOCIATION—In the case of a company limited by shares, the memorandum of association is generally accompanied by a further document, known as the Articles of Association. When registered, they become the regulations of the company, and bind every member. If there are no articles of association, the regulations contained in table A of the Companies Act 1910 are considered to be the regulations of the company; and even where there are articles of association, the provisions in table A will be applicable, unless excluded or modified by the articles. Table A may therefore be described as a model for the internal management of the company, and it deals with the transmission and transfer of shares, calls, forfeiture, the conduct of meetings, proceedings of directors, and generally with matters relating to the business of the company.

Subject to the conditions of the memorandum of association, a company's articles may always be altered by special resolution. A special resolution is one passed by a majority of not less than three-fourths of the members present in person, or by proxy, at a general meeting, of which notice specifying the intention to propose the resolution has been given, and confirmed by a majority at a subsequent meeting, held not less than fourteen days, nor more than a month, afterwards.

The articles of association cannot vary or depart from the memorandum; but in matters not required to be stated in the memorandum, the articles may supplement it. The province of the articles of association is, according to Lord Cairns, " to define the duties, the rights, and the powers of the governing body as between themselves and the company at large, and the mode and form in which the business of the company is to be carried on, and the mode and form in which changes in the internal regulations of the company may from time to time be made."

DIRECTORS—The affairs of the company are managed by directors, the number of whom is fixed by the articles of association. Under table A, the subscribers to the memorandum of association are deemed to be directors until they have determined the number and names of the first directors. After this, directors are elected at general meetings of the company. The articles usually provide that a director must possess a qualification as the holder of a certain number of shares. As a rule, they may exercise all the powers of the company, except those required to be exercised by the company in general meeting. They may enter into contracts, engage and dispense with employés, decide to pay dividends or make calls. They must keep proper books of account, and once, at least, in every year cause a balance-sheet to be prepared and laid before the members in general meeting. A copy of the balance-sheet must also be posted to the registered address of every member of the company. Directors act collectively as a board; they are agents of the company, and so long as they act bona-fidê, and without negligence, are not liable for the fraud of co-directors, nor for a breach of contract by the company. If, however, they apply the funds of the company to purposes outside the scope of the objects of the company, they are liable to repay them. The rule that an agent must not make any profit without the sanction of his principal applies to a director. He must accordingly account for any secret commission or payment from any person having trade relations with the company. So also if a director sell his own property to the company and conceals the ownership, the company, on discovering it, may rescind the contract.

PROMOTERS: PROSPECTUS—A promoter is one who busies himself or is instrumental in the formation of a company. He is usually concerned in the preparation of the prospectus. "Those who issue a prospectus," said Vice-Chancellor Kindersley, . . . "are bound to state everything with strict and scrupulous accuracy, and not only to abstain from stating as fact that which is not so, but to omit no one fact within their knowledge the existence of which might in any degree affect the nature, or extent, or quality of the privileges and advantages which the prospectus holds out as inducements to take shares."

The promoter may, of course, make a profit, but it must be disclosed to the company. The prospectus must now contain the particulars as to names and addresses of the promoters and directors, details of contracts relating to the proposed company, the amount of commission, and various other matters enumerated in section 88 of the Companies Act 1910. A prospectus which does not comply with this section is deemed to be fraudulent on the part of the promoter knowingly issuing the same. Any person fraudulently issuing a prospectus with intent to induce persons to become members of a company

is guilty of a misdemeanour, and liable to imprisonment for any term not exceeding seven years, and
to a penalty not exceeding five hundred pounds in
lieu of, or in addition to, such imprisonment. He is
also liable to pay compensation to persons misled
by the false prospectus.

SHARES—Shares are personal estate capable of
being transferred in the manner provided by the regulations of the company. A proper register of shareholders must be kept by every company; from this a
list must be forwarded annually to the Registrar-
General, containing particulars as to the capital, shareholders, shares, and calls made thereon. The register
of members is kept at the registered office of the
company, and during business hours is open to the
inspection of any member gratis, or of any other
person upon payment of one shilling.

A transfer of shares must follow the form prescribed by the articles of association; generally, it
must be executed both by the transferor and trans-
feree. The articles usually contain a provision that
the company may decline to register any transfer of
shares by a member who is indebted to it. Commonly other powers of preventing transfers are
given to the directors; but such powers must be exercised in good faith, after consideration at a board
meeting, and not without some valid reason. If the
name of any person is improperly entered or omitted
from the register of members, the party aggrieved
may proceed by motion to the Supreme Court, or
application to a judge in chambers, to have the
register rectified; and if he succeeds, the company
may be ordered to pay all the costs he has incurred.

PREFERENCE SHARES—This class of shares
is commonly met with in reconstructed companies.
In many of these preference shares were issued to
the creditors of the old company in satisfaction of
their debts; or to ordinary shareholders upon paying

up the full amount remaining uncalled upon their shares. They are also frequently issued in order to bring fresh capital into the company. The preference given to holders of these shares over ordinary shareholders may be a right to be paid first out of the capital of the company on winding-up; or a prior right to dividends; or both. The preferential nature of the shares must be expressly provided for in the memorandum or articles of association.

CALLS—In making calls the directors must follow the formalities prescribed by the articles of association. The time and place for payment must be fixed, and proper notice given. By table A it is provided that twenty-one days' notice at least must be given of every call. If the call is not paid at its due date interest may be charged at such rate as provided by the articles, or at eight per cent. under table A. If the member fail to pay on the appointed day, the directors may serve a further notice, naming a further day, on or before which the call and interest are to be paid. This notice shall also state that, in the event of non-payment, at or before the time and at the place appointed, the shares in respect of which the call was made will be liable to be forfeited.

The power of forfeiture must be exercised in good faith, and for the benefit of the company, not for the purpose of releasing a shareholder from liability. It is a strong weapon in the hands of directors, and the omission of any requirement as to giving notice or otherwise will invalidate the forfeiture; for example, forfeiture for a call not properly made, or made by directors not properly appointed, would be invalid.

Forfeited shares become the property of the company, and are disposed of according to the articles, which generally contain a provision also that any member whose shares have been forfeited shall, notwithstanding, be liable to pay all calls owing upon the shares up to the time of forfeiture.

DIVIDENDS—Dividends can only be paid out of profits, which have been defined as " the incomings after deducting the expenses of earning them." A company is not compelled, however, to make up lost capital before paying dividends, if they are properly earned as profits, and are not a payment out of capital.

CONTRACTS—Contracts on behalf of any company may be made, varied, or discharged as follows :—

(a) A contract which, if made between private persons, would be required to be in writing under seal, may be made, varied, or discharged in the name and on behalf of the company in writing under its seal.

(b) A contract required to be in writing and signed may be made, varied, or discharged in the name and on behalf of the company in writing, signed by any person acting under the express or implied authority of the company.

(c) A contract, valid although made only by parol, may be made, varied, or discharged by parol in the name and on behalf of the company by any person acting under the express or implied authority of the company.

Contracts-made by companies must, of course, be within their powers as defined by the memorandum and articles of association. If the proposed contract is within such powers, a person dealing with the company is entitled to assume that the proper requirements of form prescribed by the articles have been complied with, and is not bound to ascertain whether, for example, a proper board meeting was held, or a quorum was present when the contract was authorised.

WINDING-UP—This may be accomplished in three ways—(1) By a voluntary winding-up; (2) by a voluntary winding-up subject to the supervision of the court; and (3) by a compulsory winding-up.

A voluntary winding-up is the result of the occurrence of any event upon which it is provided by the articles that the company shall come to an end; or of a resolution by the company that it shall be wound up voluntarily. A liquidator or liquidators are appointed by the company in general meeting. The powers of the directors then cease, and the liquidator proceeds to wind up the affairs of the company and distribute its assets.

A compulsory winding-up, or winding-up by the court, is made on the petition of the company or some creditor or contributory to the Supreme Court. When a special resolution requiring the company to be wound up by the court has been passed; or when it does not commence business, or suspends business for a year; or when the number of members is reduced below five; or when the company is unable to pay its debts; or when, for numerous other reasons, the court is of opinion that the company should be wound up, it will make the order. A voluntary winding-up may be continued under the supervision of the court if the court think it desirable. If the court is of opinion that the rights of any creditor are prejudiced by a voluntary winding-up, it may order the company to be wound up by the court.

In compulsory winding-up, the liquidator is known as the official liquidator; he is appointed by, and acts under, the direction of the court, and receives such remuneration as it thinks fit. In a voluntary winding-up the liquidator receives remuneration fixed by the company, and may exercise without the sanction of the court all the powers given to the official liquidator. In a voluntary winding-up, however, the liquidator, or any creditor or contributory of the company may apply to the court to determine any question or exercise its powers in enforcing calls, or in other matters. The powers of liquidators, are very extensive, including practically everything necessary for their position as managing agent for collecting and distributing the company's assets.

The contributories of the company are those who are, or have been within a year of the winding-up, members of the company. A list of contributories is settled by the court in a compulsory winding-up, and by the liquidators in a voluntary winding-up. Every member is liable to contribute to the assets of the company to an amount sufficient for payment of the debts of the company, the cost of winding-up, and the adjustment of the rights of contributories among themselves. Calls are made by the court in compulsory, and by the liquidators in a voluntary winding-up. Contributories are of two classes, the " A " contributories being the present members of the company; the " B " list comprises those who are no longer actual shareholders. The latter are only liable if sufficient funds cannot be raised from the " A " contributories; those on the " B " list who have disposed of their shares within a year of the winding-up may then be called upon. Any " B " contributory, of course, has a right to be indemnified by the " A " contributory to whom he has transferred his shares; but such a right is in most cases of little value.

A winding-up by the court is deemed to commence at the time of the presentation of the petition for winding-up; and when an order is made, no action can be brought or continued against the company in liquidation, except by leave of the court, and subject to any terms it may impose.

In a voluntary winding-up the policy of the law is to allow the shareholders to manage their own affairs; and the court does not interfere except when called upon in the manner already indicated.

When the assets of the company have been finally collected, the debts paid so far as possible, and any surplus distributed among the shareholders, the company is dissolved. In the case of a compulsory winding-up, this is accomplished by an order of the court; in a voluntary winding-up the liquidator summons a meeting by advertisement, an account of the liquidation is given, and a return made to the Registrar-General. Then, after three months, the company automatically ceases to exist.

MINING COMPANIES—These are formed for mining purposes, the obtaining of any precious metal or mineral. They are either "limited" or "no-liability" companies. The provisions as to the limited companies are, in essentials, similar to those relating to trading companies, the chief differences being in the procedure for winding-up. In a compulsory winding-up the liquidator is appointed by the creditors, with the sanction of the court, at such remuneration as they may determine. The contributories to the assets of a mining company are the persons who, at the time of the commencement of the winding-up, are registered as holding shares in the company, and the amount of whose shares are not fully paid up.

A limited company may be formed under a system known as the prepayment system. Under this system expenditure previously incurred cannot be paid out of calls; but before each month the company estimates how much of its expenses will necessitate a call, and a call is then made to meet such estimated sum. Such a company must add to its name in the mining register book the words "Limited with prepayment."

In actual practice, however, the "No-liability" companies are those under which mining operations are usually conducted. Five per cent. of the subscribed capital must be paid up prior to registration, and a statutory declaration made by the manager verifying such payment. Any share upon which a call has been made and not paid is forfeited at' the expiration of fourteen days after the date of payment. Forfeited shares are sold by public auction, and the proceeds applied in payment of the call and the expenses of the advertisement, or other expenses in connection with the forfeiture. The balance, if any, is returned to the shareholder. Any shareholder, up to or upon the day previous to that upon which the forfeited shares are to be sold, may redeem them on payment to the manager of all calls and expenses incurred by the forfeiture.

When all the liabilities of a no-liability company have been discharged, any surplus of its property is distributed among the shareholders. After a complete distribution of the assets, the court makes an order that the company be dissolved, and directs by that order how the books and documents of the company are to be disposed of.

LIFE ASSURANCE COMPANIES AND TRUSTEE COMPANIES—The law relating to these, so far as it affects the average citizen, will be found under " Life Assurance " and " Trusts."

CONTRACTS AND AGREEMENTS.

A contract is an agreement between two or more parties by which one, at least, of them promises the other or others to do or give some particular thing, or to abstain from doing some particular act. And, generally, a valid contract may be described as an agreement enforceable by law.

A contract may be made by word of mouth, by writing, or may be inferred from the actions of the parties to it. For instance, where a person takes away an article exposed for sale in a shop with the knowledge of the shopkeeper, this constitutes an implied contract on the part of the person who takes the article to pay for it, though no word pass between him and the seller.

Contracts made by word, by writing unsealed, or implied from actions, are called "simple contracts." A contract in writing, and signed, sealed, and delivered by the parties to it, is called a deed or contract under seal. A written contract cannot be varied by "parol"—that is, by word. Verbal evidence will not be accepted in a court to vary or contradict the terms of a written agreement; but it may be admissible to supplement them when they are not clear as they stand.

CONTRACTS WHICH MUST BE IN WRITING—The law as to what contracts must be in writing is set out in an old Act of Charles the Second's time, called the "Statute of Frauds," the provisions of which are in force throughout Australia, being re-enacted by various Acts in the different States.

WRITING IS REQUIRED FOR—Any contract or sale of lands, or any interest in them, except a lease for three years or less, on which the rent is two-thirds of the annual improved value of the property.

Any agreement which is not to be performed within one year from the making thereof. This means that the parties must clearly contemplate liabilities on both sides extending beyond the year.

Any special promise to answer for the debt, default, or miscarriage of another.

A special promise by an executor or administration to answer damages out of his own estate.

Any agreement made in consideration of marriage —that is, to do or give something on account of the marriage; not a promise to marry, which may be verbal.

Any contract for the sale of goods for the price of £10 or upwards, unless the buyer accepts and actually receives part of the .goods, or gives something in part payment or to bind the bargain.

On none of these contracts can any action be brought, unless the agreement is in writing, or unless, though the contract be made by word of mouth, there is some note or memorandum of it in writing, signed by the party against whom it is attempted to enforce the contract, or by his lawfully authorised agent. Thus one party who has not signed a memorandum of the agreement, and therefore could not be sued on it, may successfully sue a party who has signed.

As to all these contracts the law seems to be, not that they are bad without writing, but only unenforceable until the necessary evidence in writing is procurable. Thus, a letter written after the contract was made, and setting out the terms of it, has been held to be a sufficient note in writing to enable the signer of it to be sued, even though in that letter he repudiated the contract. The contract being in existence, its repudiation was of no effect without the concurrence of the other party.

All contracts with regard to the sale of land, or for leases for a term of more than three years, of which a note in writing is required by the Statute of Frauds, are required by other statutes to be made by a deed under seal, or if the land is under the Transfer of Land Statute by an " instrument " which has like effect.

CONSIDERATION—Where any person sues upon a contract, unless it be made by deed, he must be prepared to show " consideration,"—that is, something given, done, suffered, or refrained from by him, in return for the promise of the other party on which he sues.

In some cases the consideration consists of a promise on the part of the person suing. For instance, A promises to marry B in consideration of B's promise to marry A. A promises to sell a horse in consideration of B promising to give £30 for it.

In other cases the consideration is not a promise to be fulfilled, but something already done by the party suing. A sues for the price of goods delivered to B, who has expressly or impliedly promised to pay for them.

If A promises to give B something without B doing, suffering, or promising anything in return, B cannot successfully sue upon the promise.

The consideration may be very small indeed, provided the law deems it of some value. Its adequacy will not usually be inquired into. That is a matter for the parties to settle for themselves, but gross inadequacy of consideration for a promise, or benefit received, may be material as evidence of fraud in securing it.

PARTIES TO A CONTRACT—All persons of full age can make contracts. Contracts made by an infant are not enforceable against him, unless they are for the supply of necessaries. What constitutes necessaries is a question of fact in each particular instance. Lunatics and drunken persons may make contracts, which can be repudiated only if at the time they made them they did not know the effect of what they were doing, and if the other party was aware of that fact.

Companies can make contracts through their properly-appointed agents.

GROUNDS FOR SETTING ASIDE CONTRACTS—Contracts may be set aside as illegal—(1) When they are in violation of morality, such as the lease of a dwelling to a woman known to be a prostitute. (2) When opposed to public policy, such as a contract not to marry, or to refrain from business in a country. A contract to refrain from business in a particular town or district is, however, good. (3) Contracts tainted with fraud. Any contract obtained by fraud may be set aside.

Misrepresentation when innocent, and mistake will sometimes, but not always, lead to the setting aside of a contract.

Where the misrepresentation refers to something which is, or should have been, within the knowledge of the party, who, however innocently mis-states, or omits to state it, the contract may be set aside. This is assuming that the misrepresentation concerns something of material importance of which a correct knowledge might have affected the making of the contract.

It is also always open to the parties to agree that the truth of some particular statement or statements shall be essential to the contract, in which case their falsity will give the party to whom they are made a right to set the agreement aside.

Mistake is a ground for setting aside a contract when it is of such a kind as to prevent any real agreement from being formed. A person, for instance, may intend to contract with a certain party, and find that he has contracted with another, with whom he would not knowingly have entered into any agreement. Again, a contract may be made with respect to a thing which has ceased to exist; or the parties, while apparently agreeing as to terms, may really mean different things. In such case mistake would vitiate the contract; but where it does not in some such way go to the root of the matter, the contract will not be affected.

REMEDIES FOR BREACH OF CONTRACT —Where one party refuses to carry out his contract, the aggrieved party may sue either for specific performance of the promise, or where performance has become impossible, or would not be ordered by the Court, for damages suffered by the failure to fulfil it.

Where any contract is broken, the plaintiff is entitled to some nominal damages; but if he has suffered no real loss, and brings a frivolous action, costs may be given against him.

DAMAGES—The rule as to measure of damages for breach of contract is that the party breaking it must pay the other party only such damages as are the natural and necessary consequence of the breach, together with all such further and other damages as, owing to the special circumstances of the particular case, must be taken to have been in the contemplation of the parties at the time when the contract was made.

The normal measure of damages for breach of promise to pay money lent is interest upon it.

For non-delivery of goods the measure of damages, when the plaintiff has not paid the price, is the difference between the contract price and the market value on or about the day of the breach of contract. But if the purchaser has made a contract for the resale of the goods, and the vendor is aware of this, the damages which he must pay may include the profits lost by the purchaser through not being able to resell, and also a portion of, or even all, the penalties which the purchaser may have to pay through not being able to deliver to the person to whom he resold.

For failure to deliver goods, which the seller knows are to be immediately used for earning money, the loss of earnings arising from the failure to deliver may be included in the damages.

For not accepting goods, the ordinary measure of damages is the difference between the price agreed on and the market price on the day the contract was broken.

Where there is a breach of warranty concerning a horse—that is, where he is warranted sound, of a certain age, etc., the purchaser is entitled to recover the whole of the price paid if the horse is returned. If the horse is not returned, the damages are the difference between the price paid and his real value; or the purchaser may resell the horse, and claim as damages the difference between what he gets for it and the price he paid.

In actions for breach of promise of marriage the damages granted have no necessary relation to the monetary loss, if any, suffered. They may be fixed at a sum which it is considered will adequately punish the defendant for faithless or heartless conduct, and act as a sufficient balm to the lacerated feelings of the plaintiff.

SPECIFIC PERFORMANCE—Specific performance means the carrying out of the terms of the contract, which may be ordered by the court in certain cases. The general rule is that damages will be granted, and specific performance will not be ordered unless performance of the thing promised is the only adequate means of doing justice to the plaintiff, and, at the same time, will not be unduly hard upon the defendant. Neither will it, as a rule, be ordered unless the court can effectually enforce the execution of its judgment.

Specific performance is much more frequently ordered of contracts with respect to land than of contracts with respect to goods. The loss of a man who has agreed to buy an estate, and whose vendor then refuses to sell, cannot be so well assessed by money in the form of damages as the loss of a man who agrees to buy other goods which he can obtain elsewhere if the vendor refuses to deliver. Should a man agree to buy any article which is unique or peculiar, so that he cannot go into the market and purchase another like it, the court will frequently order specific performance of the contract.

It will not make such an order on a contract to accept or to give personal services; nor of contracts which involve a continuous series of acts, such as contracts for the building of houses or working of mines.

Where there are any circumstances which would make the enforcement of specific performance unreasonable, the court will not grant it; nor in any case where the behaviour of the person seeking it has not been scrupulously correct in all matters relating to the contract. Lapses on his part, which might not disentitle him to damages, may prevent his obtaining an order for the defendant to carry out his promise.

When specific performance is ordered, the person who fails to comply with the order of the court is guilty of contempt, and may be punished by imprisonment.

COURTS.

JURISDICTION OF THE COURTS.

THE HIGH COURT OF AUSTRALIA—The judicial power of the Commonwealth is vested in a Federal Supreme Court, called the High Court of Australia, and in such other Courts as Parliament may invest with Federal jurisdiction. The High Court consisted, in the first instance, of a Chief Justice and two other Justices, their remuneration being £3500 for the Chief Justice, and £3000 for each of the justices. The Federal Legislature has increased the number of Judges, first to five, and afterwards to seven.

Certain actions can only be commenced i: the High Court *i.e.* in matters:

1. Arising directly under any treaty.
2. Between Commonwealth and a State.
3. Between two States.
4. Where a writ of mandamus or prohibition is sought against a Commonwealth officer or a Federal Court.

These are within the exclusive jurisdiction of the High Court. But one can always proceed in the High Court in matters:

1. Arising under any treaty.
2. Affecting consuls or other representatives of other countries.
3. In which the Commonwealth is a party.
4. Between States.
5. Between residents of different States.
6. Between a State and a resident of another State.

7. Where writ of mandamus or prohibition is sought against a Commonwealth officer.

8. Arising under the Constitution or involving its interpretation.

Except where a matter coming under these eight heads is made a matter of exclusive jurisdiction, an action may alternatively be commenced in the State Supreme Court.

APPELLATE JURISDICTION — The High Court also has power to hear appeals from any judgment of the Supreme Court of any State, whether of a single judge or of a State Full Court; and such an appeal is a matter of right where such judgment is given for a sum of the value of £300, or involves any claim or civil right amounting to £300, directly or indirectly; or where the judgment of the State Supreme Court affects the status of any person under the laws relating to aliens, marriage, divorce, or insolvency. In any other matters, whatever may be the amount involved, the High Court may, if it think fit, give special leave to appeal.

The High Court is not always the final Court of Appeal, nor is it always the only Court of Appeal. The unsuccessful litigant can ask the Privy Council for special leave to appeal from the High Court's decision. And the Privy Council can grant that leave unless the matter is a dispute between the Commonwealth and a State or between two States as to the extent of their constitutional power, in which cases there can be no appeal to the Privy Council unless the High Court certify that the matter is one which his Majesty in Council should determine.

From the Full Court one can appeal to the Privy Council:

1. As a matter of right where the subject matter exceeds £1000 in value.

2. By leave of the Privy Council in any other case.

SITTINGS—The principal seat of the High Court is to be at the seat of government; until this is established, it is held at such place as the Governor-General from time to time appoints. At the principal seat of the Court is situated the Principal Registry; and each State has a distinct registry at its seat of government. At these registries the business of the Court is carried on in the matter of issuing process, filing documents, and serving notices. The sittings of the High Court are held from time to time as required at the principal seat of the Court, and at each place where there is a district registry; at present at the capitals of each State. Usually there are three sittings of the Court at Melbourne and Sydney respectively during the year, and one or more as required at the other centres.

THE SUPREME COURT OF VICTORIA— The Supreme Court consists of judges not exceeding six in number. The term "puisne" is an old Norman French legal term, applied to all judges except the Chief, meaning, literally "younger," or inferior to the Chief Justice. The Supreme Court has complete jurisdiction in all matters civil, criminal, or mixed. It can deal with all matters in the same manner as the High Court in England in its various divisions. All ordinary trials take place before a single judge, and from his decision there is an appeal to the Full Court, which consists of not less than three of the judges sitting together. Matters preliminary to trial, and various other matters, are dealt with by a judge sitting in chambers. An elaborate code of rules of court regulates the procedure, and provides for all the necessary steps to be taken to have matters brought before and dealt with by the Court. The Court has power, subject to certain formalities, to alter and annul any rules in force, and make additional rules.

Circuits are arranged throughout the year in certain assize towns in the country, and one judge is detailed each month to conduct the business out of Melbourne.

In its criminal jurisdiction, cases are tried before a judge and jury of twelve men. In its civil jurisdiction, in actions of slander, libel, false imprisonment, malicious prosecution, seduction, or breach of promise of marriage, either party may have the trial by a jury. Equitable matters, and those requiring long examination of accounts or documents, are heard by a judge without a jury. In other matters a jury may be had on application to the Court; but otherwise every case is heard by a judge without a jury.

THE COUNTY COURT—The County Court is a Court of limited jurisdiction, and is therefore precluded from trying causes of action arising out of the State. Within the local limits of the State it has jurisdiction to hear and determine the ordinary common law actions of contract and tort where the amount sought to be recovered does not exceed £500; or actions involving any amount if both parties consent in writing to trial in the County Court. It has also jurisdiction to hear and determine actions of ejecment where the value of the premises or the rent does not exceed £50 per annum. In its equitable jurisdiction the County Court has all the powers and authority of the Supreme Court in suits by creditors, legatees, or next of kin, in which the estate involved does not exceed £500: and in suits relating to trusts, mortgages, partnerships of companies, and infants, or for specific performance of a sale, purchase, or lease, where the property does not exceed that sum.

Actions which might have been brought in the County Court may be remitted to it by the Supreme Court; and conversely in any action brought in the County Court, where the amount claimed exceeds £50, the Supreme Court may, on application, transfer it, if satisfied that the cause is one more fit to be heard in the Supreme Court. Where an action for tort or breach of promise of marriage is brought in the Supreme Court, if a judge is satisfied by affidavit that the plaintiff has no means of paying the costs of the defendant, should a verdict be found against him, he will remit the action to the County Court, unless the plaintiff give security for costs, or satisfy the judge that the cause of action is one more suitable for the Supreme Court. The procedure of the County Court is simpler, and the scale of costs less than in the Supreme Court.

Appeals may be brought by the unsuccessful party from the judgments of the County Court to the Full Court of the Supreme Court on giving security for costs of the appeal.

As in the Supreme Court, the procedure of the County Court is regulated by a compendious code of rules. Any three of the County Court judges may, under the conditions prescribed by the County Court Act, make rules for regulating the practice and procedure of the Court. In any case not provided for by the Act or rules, the general principles of practice and the rules observed in the Supreme Court may be adopted and applied with such modifications as the different constitutions of the two Courts may render necessary, at the discretion of the County Court judge before whom the matter is being tried.

County Courts are held at prescribed towns throughout Victoria. Every County Court has jurisdiction throughout the State; but provision is made for the transfer of any action to a more convenient Court than the one to which the defendant is summoned. The plaintiff should select the Court nearest to the defendant's abode or place of business, otherwise he will be non-suited if the cause of action did not arise in some material point nearer to the Court he has chosen, unless the defendant forego his right to such non-suit.

The tendency of the Legislature of late years has been to greatly increase the jurisdiction of the County Court. By the Railways Act actions against the Railways Commissioners must now be brought in the County Court, except actions for damages for sparks from engines, which are referred to arbitration. Income tax appeals and other matters are also dealt with by the County Court.

Judges of the County Court are also judges of Courts of Mines and General Sessions.

COURT OF MINES—For the purpose of carrying out the mining laws the State is divided into mining districts, and within every mining district there is a Court of Mines. This is a Court of law and equity, presided over by judges, the judges of the County Court being also appointed judges of the Court of Mines. The jurisdiction of the Court extends generally over suits concerning land in relation to mining and occupation under miners' rights, and disputes as to contracts and partnerships in relation to mining on Crown lands. An appeal lies to the Supreme Court from orders of the Court of Mines; and a judge of the Court may reserve any question in the form of a special case for the opinion of the Supreme Court. The Supreme Court gives its opinion on the special case, and a decree is made in accordance with such opinion.

THE COURT OF INSOLVENCY—The Court of Insolvency is a Court of law and equity, and, for the purpose of carrying out the matters assigned to it, has the powers, rights, incidents, and privileges of the Supreme Court. It has original jurisdiction and control in all matters of insolvency, except where the Legislature has otherwise expressly provided. It may hear and determine any matter relative to the disposition of the insolvent estate, or of any property taken under the sequestration, and claimed by the assignees or trustees for the benefit of the creditors, or relating to any acts of the assignees or trustees under the sequestration, and also in matters between the assignees or trustees and any creditor or other person appearing or otherwise submitting to the jurisdiction of the Court.

Judges of the County Court in Victoria are also judges of the Court of Insolvency. For the purposes of insolvency jurisdiction the State is divided into districts, and proceedings are usually taken and continued in the district in which the insolvent resides, unless they have been transferred by the Court to some other district. An appeal is given to the Supreme Court from orders of the Insolvency Court.

COURT OF GENERAL SESSIONS—Courts of General Sessions correspond to Courts of Quarter Sessions of the Peace in England. They are held at various places throughout the State, mentioned in the fourth schedule to the *Justices Act 1890*, on such days as the Governor-in-Council from time to time appoints. The chairman is a County Court judge, and usually sits alone; but one or more justices of the peace may sit with him. The Court hears and determines appeals from Courts of Petty Sessions against convictions, by which a penalty exceeding the sum or value of five pounds, or any term of imprisonment, has been imposed; and also against orders for committal made by a Court of Petty Sessions on fraud summons, and against orders, awarding a term of imprisonment in default of payment of a fine.

The Court of General Sessions has an extensive criminal jurisdiction. Persons committed for trial upon most indictable offences may be committed either to the Supreme Court or Court of General Sessions. Over the following offences, however, the Supreme Court alone has jurisdiction:—

(1) Treason and misprision of treason.

(2) Felonies now punishable by death.

(3) Attempts to murder.

(4) Unnatural offences.

(5) Offences against the King's title, prerogative,

person, or government, or against either House of Parliament.

(6) Bigamy and offences against the laws relating to marriage.

(7) Abduction or defilement of women or girls.

(8) Composing, printing, or publishing blasphemous, seditious, or defamatory libels.

(9) Unlawful combinations and conspiracies, except conspiracies and combinations to commit any offence, which Courts of General Sessions have jurisdiction to try when committed by one person.

(10) Offences which by any Act cannot be prosecuted or tried at any Court of General Sessions.

(11) Unlawfully and maliciously setting fire to any property under such circmstances as make such act a capital offence.

LICENSING COURT—For the purposes of carrying out the licensing law Victoria is divided into licensing districts, proclaimed by the Governor-in-Council and notified by name in the " Government Gazette." For every licensing district there is a Licensing Court, held at such intervals as the Governor-in-Council from time to time, by notice in the " Government Gazette," appoints. All judges of County Courts and all police magistrates are licensing magistrates for every licensing district. A Licensing Court is composed of any three licensing magistrates; but in the Metropolitan, Ballarat, and Sandhurst groups of licensing districts, and elsewhere for certain matters, such as cases involving the payment of compensation, one of the licensing magistrates must be a County Court judge. Any one member of a Licensing Court is deemed to constitute a Court for certain matters of procedure preliminary to the hearing of applications, and after the hearing for issuing the necessary process to enforce the adjudication of the Court. He may also give permission for a change in the name of licensed premises, and approve of a manager being appointed until the next annual sitting of the Licensing Court, and hear unopposed applications for transfer or renewals of licenses. The summons or warrant of any Licensing Court may be served or executed within any part of Victoria.

The Licensing Court has exclusive jurisdiction to hear and determine all cases concerning the granting or refusing of licenses for hotels, renewals of licenses, revocation, forfeiture, or cancellation of licenses, appeals from the orders of licensing inspectors, disqualification of licensed persons and premises, and the determination as to which licensed premises in any district shall be deprived of a license in consequence of the determination of the electors.

Any person aggrieved by the determination of any Licensing Court may require a case to be stated for the opinion of the Supreme Court, which then determines the questions of law arising on the case. The Supreme Court may reverse, affirm, or amend the determination of the Licensing Court, or remit the matter to the Licensing Court, with its opinion, or make such other order as it shall think fit. Security must be given by any appellant on applying to have a case stated; and no greater sum than twenty pounds is allowed for costs to any appellant if successful in his appeal.

At present the Licensing Court for each district holds its annual sitting in December.

COURTS OF PETTY SESSIONS AND JUSTICES.

Justices of the Peace are appointed by commission under the seal of the State. The President of a shire and the Mayor of a city, town, or borough, and the Mayor and Mayor-Elect for the time being of the city of Melbourne and town of Geelong, are justices while they hold such positions. Justices are appointed to officiate in the bailiwicks in which they reside. Members of the Executive Council, chairmen of General Sessions, coroners, deputy coroners, and police magistrates are justices for every bailiwick, unless prohibited from so acting by order published in the " Government Gazette." A justice who becomes insolvent vacates his office.

Police magistrates are salaried officers appointed under the *Public Service Act*, and are now invariably appointed from the civil service.

A Court of Petty Sessions is composed of two or more justices, or a police magistrate alone. If the bench be composed of a police magistrate and other justices, their powers are equal; but the police magistrate acts as chairman of the bench. A single honorary justice may constitute a Court of Petty Sessions if both parties to the proceeding consent in writing.

The jurisdiction of the Court of Petty Sessions is undoubtedly more often called into requisition than that of any other tribunal. On the criminal side it commits for trial or discharges, and accepts or refuses bail to persons accused of indictable offences. It has also a summary jurisdiction over numerous offences conferred by various Acts of Parliament. In its civil jurisdiction, where the sum claimed does not exceed fifty pounds, it may hear and determine the various causes of action enumerated in the *Justices Act 1890,* section 59, as amended by the *Justices Act 1904,* No. 1959, section 14.

A justice out of Sessions has also extensive powers conferred by the common law and by various statutes. Among others, he may receive informations in respect of offences and complaints in civil matters, and issue his summons thereon; or, where the information is on oath, his warrant to apprehend. He may also issue search warrants, summon witnesses, and do all necessary acts preliminary to the hearing. He may commit persons accused of indictable offences for trial, and accept or refuse bail. A very important

function of a justice is that of holding an inquest, if
requested by a police officer in charge of a station or a
coroner; in doing so, he has the full jurisdiction of
a coroner.   A justice is not, however, compelled to
perform this duty against his will.

An appeal from the summary convictions of Courts
of Petty Sessions and justices, in certain cases, lies
to the Court of General Sessions.   [See *Court of
General Sessions.*]

In civil matters, and in summary convictions or
orders, or in the issuing of a warrant where the Court
of Petty Sessions or justices have made an error in law,
the person aggrieved may apply within a month to
a Supreme. Court judge for an order to review the
decision.   In the case of a civil debt, however, if
the amount does not exceed five pounds, the judge
will not grant an order to review the decision,
even though it is erroneous, unless it involves some
public matter of law or of general application, or some
undecided question of law; or unless the Court of
Petty Sessions or justice had no jurisdiction to make
the order, and the order so made is substantially
unjust.   The judge appoints a day when the order
to review is returnable, and the person in whose
favour the original order of the Court of Petty Sessions or justice was made may then show cause why
this should not be set aside.   The judge may then
affirm or reverse the order complained of, or
remit the matter for re-hearing, and make such order
as to costs as it thinks fit. The costs awarded in any
order to review are limited to twenty pounds.   Where
the Court of Petty Sessions or justice have decided a
question purely of fact, the judge, on an order
to review, will not interfere with their finding, although it would, on the facts proved, have come to a
different conclusion, unless there was really no evidence upon which such finding could have been based.

 The statutory order to review is the process most
generally used to rectify the erroneous decisions in

law of Courts of Petty Sessions and justices. The Supreme Court, however, has a general control over all inferior tribunals in certain cases by *prohibition, certiorari*, and *mandamus*. [See *Glossary of Legal Terms.*] Where a justice refuses to do any act relating to the duties of his office, the Supreme Court may also issue a *mandatory order*. The procedure in relation to such order is similar to that upon an order to review. An *order nisi* is granted, calling upon the justice and the party to be affected by the act to show cause why such act should not be done. On the day appointed for the hearing, the Supreme Court may make the order *absolute*, when the justice must obey it, and do the act required; or discharge the order *nisi*, and make such order as to costs as it thinks fit. There can be no appeal to the Full Court from the Judge's dismissal of the order to review, but the High Court will, if it thinks the matter sufficiently important, grant special leave to appeal.

CORONER'S COURT—The office and jurisdiction of the coroner is one of the most ancient in English law, dating back long before Magna Charta. He has jurisdiction both by the common law and by statute. His Court is a Court of Record, and he has power to commit for contempt. His functions are to enquire concerning the manner of the death of any person who is slain or drowned, or who dies suddenly, or in prison, or while detained in any lunatic asylum, or whose body shall be lying dead within his district; and to enquire into the cause and origin of any fire, whereby any building, ship, or merchandise, or stack of corn, pulse, or hay, or growing crop is destroyed or damaged.

A jury is not necessary unless the Attorney-General or any Act of Parliament expressly directs the inquest to be by jurors. Jurors are summoned either verbally or by precept by the coroner who may fine any one refusing to serve a sum not exceeding £5. The number of jurors is not less than five nor

more than twelve; and a verdict of a majority is taken
as the verdict of all.   If a majority do not agree
after two hours deliberation, the coroner may discharge the jury, and proceed to hold another inquest
with a fresh jury.   Where a coroner's jury has found
against anyone a verdict of manslaughter or wilfully
firing any ship or other property, the coroner may,
if he thinks fit, accept bail for the accused's appearance at the next criminal sittings of the Supreme
Court or at the Court of General Sessions.

Every licensed victualler must, at the request of the
police, receive into his house any dead body for the
purpose of an inquest being held.

Coroners are appointed by the Governor-in-Council,
who also appoints the districts within which the
coroner so appointed shall act.

WARDEN'S COURTS—Police magistrates are
appointed "Wardens of the Gold Fields," and have
jurisdiction in the various districts for which they have
been appointed.   Every warden has jurisdiction to
hear suits relating to the matters previously mentioned
under *The Court of Mines*, and, in addition, numerous
matters set out in the Mines Acts.   The jurisdiction
is of a very special and technical nature, the details
of which can only be acquired by a careful persual
of the *Mines Act 1890*, and the various amendments
thereof.   The decisions of the warden are reviewed
by appeal to the Court of Mines, and by case stated
to the Supreme Court.

DISTRIBUTION OF ESTATES OF INTESTATES.

When a person dies intestate, that is, without having made a valid testamentary document, his property is distributed according to certain rules of law, most of which date from the time of Charles II., when the Statute of Distributions (22 and 23 Car. II. c. 10) was passed. Important modifications have, however, been made from time to time.

In order to deal with the estate of an intestate, an administrator must be appointed by the court. [See *Probate and Administration.*] As soon as letters of administration are granted the property of the deceased vests in the administrator, who must then pay the debts of the deceased. It is presumed that an administrator will have fully informed himself of the state of the property after one year. Accordingly, he could not be compelled to distribute the estate among those entitled before that period has elapsed. For the purpose of distributing the property he must sell land and other assets, turning everything into money, unless all those interested agree among themselves on a scheme of distribution which does not involve sale, and give proper indemnity to the administrator for not selling and dividing the money which would have been realised.

PER STIRPES—PER CAPITA—After the payment of debts and expenses of administration, the surplus of the estate of an intestate goes as to one-third to his widow, the remaining two-thirds to his children. Where there is no widow, but only children, the estate is distributable among the children equally. If any of his children have predeceased him, leaving children, the latter tak· the parent's share. The technical name for the right in which the grandchildren of an intestate take the share their parent would have taken if alive, is *per stirpes*, the parent being the stirps or root of their inheritance. The children of an intestate, on the other hand, take *per capita*, literally, by heads, each having an equal share. The difference may be shown practically as follows:—John Jones dies intestate, leaving three children, William, James, and Mary; a fourth child, Elizabeth, died before him, leaving six children. John Jones' estate would be distributed in four equal parts, William, James, and Mary each taking one-fourth; while the remaining fourth would be distributed equally between the six children of Elizabeth. Elizabeth's children take their mother's share *per stirpes;* as between themselves, it is distributed equally among them.

HOTCHPOT—The Statute of Distributions provides that no child of the intestate, except his heir-at-law, who shall have any estate in land by the settlement of the intestate, or who shall be advanced in his lifetime by pecuniary portion, shall share in the distribution unless the portion already obtained is brought into hotchpot. The meaning of this is, that if a father has already given a portion—that is, such a provision as he might have been expected to make after his death for any child during his lifetime, it would be inequitable to allow that child to come in on equal terms with the other children as to the rest of his property. That child must accordingly either rest content with the share already got, or put its value into a general pool, so to speak, with the rest of the property, and then receive back the difference between the amount of the share already obtained and the full share of each child in the whole property. This provision applies only to intestate fathers; so that if a mother dies intestate leaving children, a child who has received a portion during the mother's lifetime need not bring it into hotchpot.

SHARE OF THE WIDOW—If the intestate left a widow, but no children, or representatives of children, the widow was formerly entitled to one-half, and the other one-half went to the " next of kindred of the intestate, who are in equal degree, and those who legally represent them," i.e., their offspring or descendants. In 1896, however, the *Intestates Estates Act* in Victoria made an important modification in favour of the widow. If the estate does not exceed £1000, and there are no children, the estate belongs to the widow absolutely and exclusively. Where the estate exceeds £1000, the widow still has a charge on the whole estate for £1000, with interest from the death of her husband at four per cent. until payment; and, in addition to this, is entitled to share in the residue of the estate after deducting the £1000, as if such residue had been the whole estate—that is, she will take one-half of the remainder, and one-half will go to the next-of-kin.

This provision in favour of the widow only, not the widower, has been held to refer only to the case of a total intestacy. Accordingly, if a man made a will, which was duly proved, and it should turn out that part of his estate had not been disposed of by the will, it seems that the widow's prior right to the £1000 would not apply.

An only child would take two-thirds if the intestate left a widow; otherwise, the whole. A posthumous child is in the same position as one born in the parent's lifetime; and brothers and sisters of the half-blood share equally with the others,

NEXT-OF-KIN—The method employed in order to ascertain the legal next-of-kin is to count up or down, as the case may be, to the person to whom relationship is sought from the person

who claims to be kindred with him or her.
Each step counts as one degree. For example,
John Jones dies intestate. His father and his
son are related to him in the first degree, each
being one step from him; a brother and grandfather
in the second degree, and so on.

If the intestate therefore leave neither children nor
parents, but brothers and sisters, and a grandfather,
then, since they are all in the same degree, they should,
in strictness, be entitled equally. But from an early
period the courts in England preferred the brothers
and sisters. Accordingly, they take to the exclusion
of a grandfather or grandmother. A grandfather
would, however, take to the exclusion of an uncle,
who is in the third degree.

The mother also is in the same degree of kinship
as the father; but by a statute of James II. she is only
entitled to share with the intestate's brothers and
sisters.

A detailed enumeration of the various contingencies could not be here attempted; but the subjoined
list will show the more common examples:—

If a person dies intestate leaving—	His property is thus disposed of—
Widow and Children	One-third to Widow, two-thirds to Children.
Widow	All if estate is under £1000; if more than £1000, Widow receives £1000 and half the balance, the other half going to the next-of-kin.
Father	All.
Mother	All.
Brothers and Sisters	All equally. If a Brother or Sister be dead, leaving Children, they take their parent's share.
Father and Brothers and Sisters; or Father and Mother and Brothers and Sisters	The Father takes all.

Mother and Brothers and Sisters	All share equally.
Mother and Children of deceased Brother	The Mother takes one-half; the Children of deceased Brother one-half between them.
Grandfather and Brothers and Sisters	Brothers and Sisters take all equally.
Uncle and Nephews	All equally.
Child or Children	All to the Child or equally among the Children.
Children by two Wives	Equally among all.
Husband	One-half; the other half to next-of-kin.
Husband and Children	One-third to Husband; two-thirds to Children.
Mother only	All to her.
Uncle or Aunt's Children and Brother's or Sister's Grandchildren	All equally.
Uncle and Child of deceased Uncle	All to Uncle.
Nephew by Brother and Nephew by Half-brother	Equally to both.
Children of deceased Brothers or Sisters	Equally among all.

MAINTENANCE OF WIDOW AND CHILDREN.—Though a husband or father may make a will entirely or partially disinheriting his wife or child, yet the Supreme Court, acting under the "Widows and Young Children's Maintenance Act 1906," may vary the will so as to allow to wife or child such yearly income as it thinks sufficient for maintenance of wife or child.

DIVORCE.

A male petitioner must always be domiciled in Victoria—that is, he must have such a connection with Victoria that it is, in the eye of the law, the place which he intends as his permanent home. A wife is deemed to have her husband's domicile, and consequently both Parliament and the Courts have been compelled to make an exception in the case of the woman whose husband has deserted her. She may petition here if at the time of desertion her husband is domiciled here. The reason we insist on domicil is that by international law, a foreign court will recognise a divorce only if it is pronounced by the Court of domicile.

Under the "Shiels Act"—*Marriage Act 1890, sec. 74*—it is not enough to be domiciled. The domicil must have existed two years and the petitioner must not have come to Victoria for the purpose only of petitioning.

GROUNDS OF DIVORCE—By the "Shiels Act" a marriage may be dissolved upon the grounds—(1) That the respondent has, without just cause or excuse, wilfully deserted the petitioner, and left him or her so deserted during three years and upward. (2) That the respondent has, during three years and upwards, been an habitual drunkard, and either habitually left his wife without support, or been guilty of cruelty towards her; or, being the petitioner's wife, has for the same period been an habitual drunkard, and habitually neglected her domestic duties, or rendered herself unfit to discharge them. (3) On the ground that, at the time of the presentation of the petition, the respondent has been imprisoned for a period of not less than three years, and is still in prison under a commuted sentence for a capital crime, or under sentence to penal servitude for seven years or upwards; or, being a husband, has within five years undergone frequent convictions for crime, and been sentenced, in the aggregate, to imprisonment for three years or upwards, and left his wife without support. (4) On the ground that, within one year previously, the respondent has been convicted of having attempted to murder the petitioner, or of having assaulted him or her with intent to inflict grievous bodily harm; or on the ground that the respondent has repeatedly during that period assaulted and cruelly beaten the petitioner. (5) On the ground that the respondent, being a husband, has since his marriage and the eighth day of May, 1890, been guilty of adultery in the conjugal residence, or coupled with circumstances or conduct of aggravation; or of a repeated act of adultery.

If, in the opinion of the court, the petitioner's own habits induced or contributed to the wrong complained of, the petition may be dismissed; but otherwise the court will pronounce a decree dissolving the marriage.

These grounds of divorce were introduced in 1889. Prior to this, a marriage could be dissolved for the following reasons, which are still applicable in addition to those above given:—(6) A husband may present a petition for dissolution on the ground that the wife has, since the marriage, been guilty of adultery. (7) A wife may present a petition for dissolution on the ground that, since the marriage, the husband has been guilty of incestuous adultery, or of bigamy with adultery, or of rape, or of sodomy, or bestiality, or of adultery with desertion for two years or upwards; or of such cruelty as, without adultery, would have entitled her to a judicial separation in England at the time the Act came into force (1865).

PROCEDURE—When a petition is presented by a husband on the ground of misconduct, the petitioner must make the alleged adulterer a co-respondent, unless he applies, and is allowed by the court on special grounds, to be excused from so doing. This is usually done when he is unable to identify the person. When a petition is presented by a wife, the court, if it see fit, may direct that the person with whom the husband is alleged to have committed adultery be made a respondent.

The court must be satisfied of the absence of collusion between the parties, and also that the petitioner has not connived at the wrong complained of, or condoned it. Condonation consists in resuming marital relations, with full knowledge of the offence committed by the guilty party.

A law officer, if he think fit, may oppose the petition; and, by leave of the court, any other person may oppose a petition presented on the ground of adultery on showing, by affidavit, that there is reason to believe that petitioner has been accessory to, or connived at, the adultery.

DECREE—Every decree for a divorce in the first instance is a *decree nisi*, which is not made *absolute* till after the expiration of such time, not less than three months, as the court may direct. A *decree nisi* means, literally, " a decree unless " some cause is shown why it should not be made absolute. After the expiration of the three months, or such time as may have been directed, the decree is made absolute by the Prothonotary of the Supreme Court on a request in writing by the petitioner if no matter in oppositon is then pending. During the period between the pronouncing of the decree *nisi* and the time for issuing the decree *absolute*, any person may, if the court think fit, be allowed to show cause why the decree should not be made absolute, if it was obtained by collusion, or by reason of the suppression of material facts. At any time during the progress of the cause, or before the decree is made absolute, any person may give information to the Attorney-General of any matter material to the case. The Attorney-General may then intervene if he suspect a decree is being obtained contrary to the justice of the case, and call witnesses to prove the grounds upon which he has intervened. The court then rehears the case, and either confirms or reverses its previous decision according to the facts proved, providing for the costs of the intervention as it sees fit.

On every decree *nisi* a notice is indorsed that, if the petitioner or respondent shall contract marriage before the decree is made absolute, he or she shall be guilty of bigamy. After the decree is made absolute either party is free to marry again.

Parties frequently neglect to have the decree made absolute, and should be careful to do so. On a request in writing it will be issued as a matter of course.

The court is not bound to pronounce a decree if, during the marriage, the petitioner has been guilty of adultery, or of unreasonable delay in presenting the petition, or of cruelty towards the other party, or of having deserted or wilfully separated himself or herself from the other party before the adultery complained of, or of such other wilful neglect or misconduct as has conduced to the adultery; or, as previously stated, if the petitioner's own conduct has induced the wrong complained of.

ALIMONY—The court may order a gross or annual sum of money to be paid by a husband, and cause a proper deed to be settled and executed by the necessary parties. A wife who is petitioner may be allowed alimony during the suit, or *pendente lite*, in the technical language of the law. A wife who is respondent, after entering an appearance to the suit.

may apply for, and be allowed, a reasonable sum for alimony during the suit.   Where permanent alimony has been allowed against a husband who is respon- dent, the court may modify or discharge its order for alimony if he is unable to make the payments. Where the wife has married again, or if there be any other just cause for so doing, the court may dis- charge the order for alimony; or if there 1 e infant children in her custody, may vary the order.

DOGS.

Every owner of a dog in Victoria must register it within fifteen days after the first day of March in every year, or within six months from the day on which the dog was littered. Registration consists in delivering a description setting forth certain particulars required by the *Dog Act 1890*, and in paying to the registration officer a fee of five shillings. When the first registration is made after the first of September in any year only half a crown is payable. The registration officer is required to keep a correct list of the names of owners, and the numbers of the dogs, with their registered number. Any person, on payment of the sum of one shilling, can obtain particulars of any dog so registered from the registration officer. Any person neglecting to register, or knowingly making a false declaration, is liable to penalties. Every registered dog, except foxhounds, beagles, and greyhounds, engaged in public coursing matches, should have a collar round its neck, with the words " Registered at " the place of its registration, and the name and address of its owner. If such a dog is found wandering at large, the police or the officers of the municipality may seize it, and give notice in writing within forty-eight hours to the owner. If the owner does not reclaim it within forty-eight hours after the delivery of the notice, and pay the sum of two shillings and sixpence, the dog may be sold by auction, or destroyed without cruelty. If a dog is found wandering at large without a collar containing the particulars above-mentioned, it may be sold by auction or destroyed, unless the owner, within forty-eight hours, claim it and pay the sum of two shillings and sixpence, together with twice the registration fee in case such dog is not registered. Particulars as to registration may be obtained from the council of any municipality, whose duty it is to appoint a proper officer to carry out the provisions of the Act.

Any person wilfully removing a collar from a registered dog is liable to a penalty not exceeding five pounds. The owner of any slut at large in any public highway while on heat is liable to a similar penalty. The owner or occupier of any paddock enclosed by a fence, in which sheep, cattle, or poultry are confined, may destroy any dog found at large therein, unless it is accompanied by its owner or some other person. If any person wilfully urge any dog to attack anyone, or any horse, sheep, poultry, or cattle, he is liable on conviction to a penalty not exceeding twenty pounds, or to be imprisoned for any term not exceeding three months.

DAMAGE BY DOGS—If any dog rush at any person, or any horse, cattle, or sheep, the owner is liable to a penalty of not more than five pounds. In addition to this penalty, the person attacked, or the owner of the horse, cattle, or sheep, may recover compensation for the amount of actual damage done by the dog. In this case, it is not necessary to prove that the owner of the dog knew its mischievous disposition. This provision applies only to proceedings before justices under the Act. If an action is brought in the Supreme Court or County Court to recover damages for injuries inflicted by a dog, it is necessary to prove that the owner knew its mischievous tendencies. This is technically known as the doctrine of "*scienter*," the theory of the law being that, until a dog has had "his first bite," the owner cannot be supposed to know that he is of a dangerous disposition. Very slight evidence will be sufficient to show that the ferocious nature of a dog was known to its owner. It is generally safer for the injured party, however, to adopt the procedure of the Act, and proceed before justices to recover the "actual damage," because the knowledge of the owner of the dog of its vicious propensities then becomes immaterial. Under the head of "actual damage," the injured party is entitled to recover the monetary loss he has incurred in consequence of the bite. These would include medical expenses, if he is personally injured, or the cost of veterinary attendance upon an injured animal, or its value if destroyed.

Greyhounds must not be trained within the limits of any city, town, or borough, except upon private property, unless such greyhound be muzzled.

The Act does not apply to any dog bona-fidê kept and used as a guide for any blind person, provided that the dog be registered. No fee is charged for the registration of such a dog.

The owner of a dog is not liable if the person bitten be a trespasser—that is, a person not lawfully upon the premises by the permission or at the invitation of the owner of the premises.

DOMESTIC SERVANTS.

Domestic servants are those employed in a house, or in performing personal services for the employer. Grooms and gardeners are domestic servants; but a governess or tutor is not.

In the event of wilful disobedience to a lawful order of the master or mistress, or in the case of misconduct, dishonesty, drunkenness, or permanent disablement, a servant may be dismissed without notice, or wages in lieu of notice.

An employer is not entitled to deduct anything from a servant's wages for breakages, unless there has been an agreement to that effect. In an action brought against him for wages, however, he might be entitled to counter-claim for the amount.

The length of notice necessary to terminate the employment on either side will depend on the agreement between the parties. In the case of domestic servants, a week's notice is that most usually adopted. Where there is no express stipulation, a reasonable notice must be given. In England a domestic servant is by custom entitled to give and receive a month's notice where there is no express agreement. In Australia, however, it is probable that a week's notice would be that implied in the majority of cases, except where the servant is employed in distant parts or places to which access is difficult and expensive, or, from other circumstances, it is to be inferred that a longer notice was contemplated.

Where a servant leaves without notice, or is dismissed for wilful disobedience or misconduct, the wages accruing from the last payment up to the time of leaving or dismissal are forfeited. If a servant is wrongfully dismissed, he or she is entitled to wages for the time of notice that should have been given. The death of either party puts an end to the contract of service; but a servant is entitled to wages up to the time of death of the employer.

A servant is not entitled to demand a character from his or her employer.

EXECUTORS.

An executor is the person appointed by a will to carry out its provisions. One or more executors may be appointed, and they may be either individuals or certain companies which are authorised by statute to act as executors.

An executor must bury the deceased in a manner suitable to the estate he leaves, or in accordance with any special instructions contained in the will. Reasonable funeral expenses take precedence of all other debts and charges.

The executor must take out probate of the will, make an inventory of the deceased's property, for which purpose he may employ a valuer. He must pay the debts of the deceased so far as the estate will do it, and collect debts owing to the deceased, taking legal action to recover them when it is necessary. After payment of the debts, he must pay the legacies given by the will, reducing them proportionately when there is not enough to meet them all.

Any property which is not specifically given to any person may be sold by the executor to provide funds for the payment of legacies, but a specific gift, as, for instance, of a house, a farm, or a specially designated fund, such as the money standing to the credit of the deceased in a certain bank, cannot be sold or used to provide for payment of other legacies.

Nor can such specific gifts be used for the payment of debts until the residue of the estate and general money legacies have been exhausted.

An executor is liable, as far as the estate of the deceased will meet them, on all contracts made by the testator which are not strictly personal, such as a contract to marry, contracts of agency, and of personal service.

An executor is given ample discretion in paying or allowing claims made against the estate, and in pressing or compounding, settling or abandoning the claims of the deceased against others. He is bound to use reasonable care and judgment, and to do what he considers best for the estate.

Sometimes an executor is an infant—that is, under the age of 21 years on the testator's death—in which case he is unable to act until of full age, an administrator appointed by the court acting in the meantime.

Where there is more than one executor, all must be joined as plaintiffs in bringing any action with regard to the estate.

One executor of several can give a receipt, and it is not necessary for all to join.

An executor is bound to twice file accounts of the estate in the Supreme Court ; first, within three months of the grant of probate, on which occasion he must present a statement of the assets and liabilities of the deceased ; and, second, fifteen months after the granting of probate. He is then required to file accounts showing how he has dealt with the estate. His duties may continue for long after this, but he is not required to present further accounts to the court unless specially ordered to do so. He, however, is always liable to account to the persons interested in the estate, to whom he is in the position of a trustee.

If any question arise affecting the estate which the executor is unable to determine, or which might involve him in risk if he acted upon his own responsibility, he may apply by a procedure, known as an Originating Summons, to the Supreme Court for the determination of the question. He should serve the summons upon all parties whose interests may be affected. If the matter is a proper one to bring before the court—that is, unless the application is merely frivolous and unnecessary, and made for the purpose of running up costs—the court directs the executor in the matter, and orders all the costs of the parties to be paid out of the estate.

[*See further Probate and Administration.*]

FIRE INSURANCE.

Fire insurance differs in an important respect from life insurance, the latter providing for the payment of a specified sum on death, and the former merely providing that the insurance company will make good the loss or damage which the person insuring may sustain by fire.

Thus, an insurance company, instead of paying the money for which a house is insured, may, if it choose, repair or rebuild it.

Truthful description of the premises is required from the insurer, and there is an implied engagement on his part that he will not alter them in any such way as to increase the risk of fire. If he does so to any material extent the policy will be vitiated. Therefore notice should always be given to the insurance office of any alteration of the premises; but a mere change in the use to which they are put, if it does not involve any increased risk from fire, will not necessarily vitiate the policy.

The burning of a house which is let does not relieve the tenant of his liability to pay rent, whether the premises are insured or uninsured. In leases for any considerable length of time the tenant is usually required to insure the premises in the name of the owner.

Where furniture is insured, the policy protects it only so long as it remains in the house where it was when insured. Therefore notice should be given on its removal, so that the policy may be altered.

Notice of loss of insured property by fire should be given promptly, with particulars of the damage suffered.

The damage resulting from a bona-fidê attempt to put out the fire and to save goods is considered as damage by fire, and insurance may be claimed thereon. Goods, for instance, which are spoilt by water, used by the inmates of the house, or by the fire brigade, or by being thrown out of the window to prevent their burning, are covered by the insurance of them.

FIRMS' REGISTRATION.

A " firm " means any two or more persons lawfully associated for the purpose of carrying on any business. The " firm-name " is the name or style under which any business is carried on.

In Victoria every firm carrying on business, or having any place of business, under a firm-name, which does not consist of the full or the usual names of all the partners, without any addition; and every person carrying on business, or having any place of business, under any firm-name, consisting of or containing any name or addition, other than the full or usual name of that person, must register the name under which the business is to be carried on. This provision does not apply to temporary contractors, who do not publicly notify themselves as regularly carrying on business in Victoria.

Registration is effected by delivering to the Registrar-General a statement in writing, containing the firm-name, the place of business, the nature of the business, the full name, usual residence, and other occupation (if any) of the person or persons carrying on or intending to carry on the business; and if the business is commenced, or a new place of business established, after the date of *The Registration of Firms Act,* September 1st, 1892, the date of commencement of the business, or of the establishment of the place of business.

The firm-name registered under the Act must be used in all matters relating to the business. Where a change occurs in the constitution of a registered firm the members of the reconstituted firm, within a month, must notify the Registrar-General in the form prescribed by the Act. When the name is changed the firm must be registered as if it were a new firm, and in the statement to the Registrar-General the former name must be mentioned as having been abandoned.

Any person making default without reasonable excuse in registering may become liable to a penalty of five pounds for the first offence, and ten pounds for every subsequent conviction.

Where an action has been commenced in the firm-name or for a cause of action relating to the firm by any unregistered firm or person, that should have been registered, the Court will order the firm, or person in default, to register; it may also stay all proceedings in the action till the order be complied with, or allow the action to proceed on an undertaking that registration will be effected within a time to be named.

Any person wilfully making a false statement to the Registrar-General is guilty of a misdemeanour, and on conviction liable to imprisonment for a term not exceeding two years.

The Registrar-General keeps a register and index of all the firms and firm-names registered and all statements relating thereto. Any person, on payment of one shilling, may inspect and take copies from this. A certificate of registration or copy of a registered statement, purporting to be signed and certified by the Registrar-General, is *prima-faciê* evidence in any Court of the fact and date of registration. The details of the forms of statements and notices required, and fees payable, may be obtained at the office of the Registrar-General.

The object of the Act is to give reliable information to the public of the names of the persons with whom they enter into business relations. Consequently, when a person trades under his own name, or a firm under the usual names of all the partners, there is no necessity for registration.

HOTELKEEPERS AND TRAVELLERS.

The legal definition of an inn is " a house where the traveller is furnished with everything he has occasion for while on his way." Every house for which a victualler's licence is granted is a common inn. A hotelkeeper, anciently known as hosteler or hostler, is one who makes it his business to entertain travellers. He is bound to supply at reasonable prices lodging and refreshment to every person who applies, if there is room, and such person is sober and orderly. The intending lodger must tender payment if required; and if he should come in such a condition, or so conduct himself as to be offensive to the other inmates, he need not be received. If all the bedrooms should be occupied, the hotelkeeper is not bound to take in a traveller and allow him to sleep in a sitting-room. A traveller is not entitled, except by special agreement, to remain indefinitely. As soon as he has lost the character of a " traveller " he may be required to leave on receiving reasonable notice.

HOTELKEEPER'S RESPONSIBILITY—It is the duty of the hotelkeeper to keep safely the property of the lodger or guest; but he is not responsible for the safe custody of any goods or chattels the property of any lodger or guest above the value of ten pounds, unless they have been given into his charge. In the case of goods of a certain nature, specified in the *Carriers and Innkeepers Act 1890*, such as gold, jewellery, pictures, plate, silks, etc., contained in any package the value of which exceeds ten pounds, the hotelkeeper is not responsible for loss or injury to them unless the value and nature of the articles have been declared, and any increased charge, which he is authorised to make for their

custody, paid or assented to. Usually hotelkeepers
do not require extra payment, but notify by a conspicuous notice, in a prominent part of the premises,
the conditions under which such goods are received.
If injury or loss to the lodger's goods is occasioned
by the act of God, or the negligence of the lodger
himself, the hotelkeeper is not liable. What would
amount to negligence would be a question of fact
depending on the circumstances of the case.

The goods of a lodger or guest cannot be distrained upon for rent due by the hotelkeeper. The
latter is entitled, however, to a general lien upon all
goods for the amount due for board and lodging;
and this extends to articles not strictly the property of a lodger, such as a commercial traveller's
samples. This lien is not lost by an occasional
absence of the lodger; but if he is permitted to take
away the goods, and returns subsequently, the hotelkeeper will have no longer any lien for the amount
due in respect of his former stay. Luggage or goods
left at an hotel where the owner is not staying, and
not paid for, would not be in the custody of the hotelkeeper as such.

LICENSED VICTUALLERS—A hotelkeeper in
Victoria is known as a licensed victualler, and,
in order to carry on his occupation, he must
obtain a license under the Licensing Act. This
authorises the licensed person to sell liquor in any
quantity upon the premises between the hours of
six in the morning and half-past eleven at night. By
special permit from the Licensing Court, licensed
victuallers in the neighbourhood of wharves, markets,
cattle or sheep yards, abattoirs, or railway and
coach stations, may sell liquor before and after these
hours. Every licensed person must keep his name
on the front of his premises, with the word
"licensed" or other words sufficient to show the
nature of his business. He may not permit unlawful

games, or suffer prostitutes, thieves, or drunken and disorderly persons to be on his premises. Where a license is granted in respect of a hotel to be provided with stabling, a sufficient supply of hay and corn must be kept for travellers. Except in places lighted by the ratepayers, the licensed victualler must keep a lamp lighted near the principal entrance from sunset to sunrise. He must not supply liquor to intoxicated persons, or aborigines, or habitual drunkards in regard to whom justices have made an order prohibiting persons supplying them with liquor; or to any person apparently under the age of sixteen for consumption on the premises. For the sale of liquor he must not receive payment otherwise than in money, cheques, or money-orders. He cannot sue for liquor supplied for consumption on the premises, except that supplied with meals to a bona-fidê lodger. Lodgers may be served with liquor on Sunday; but the hotelkeeper is not bound to serve them. No other person may be served upon Sunday, except a bona-fidê traveller. A bona-fidê traveller is one who resides at least ten miles away, and has travelled that distance. A person who falsely represents himself to be a bona-fidê traveller, or lodger, for the purpose of being supplied with liquor, is liable to penalties.

By the Health Acts of Victoria any person who knowingly lets a part of a house in which someone has been suffering from a contagious or infectious disease, without obtaining a certificate from a legally qualified medical practitioner that it has been disinfected to his satisfaction, is liable to penalties; so, also, is any person who, in letting or showing part of a house for the purpose of letting it, answers falsely any question as to the fact of there having been within six weeks previously any occupant suffering from such disease. A hotelkeeper " lets part of a house " to any person admitted as a guest into his licensed premises.

HUSBAND AND WIFE.

Marriage has been judicially defined as "the voluntary union for life of one man and one woman to the exclusion of all others." Mr. Bishop, a leading authority, regards it as "the civil status of one man and one woman united in law for life under the obligations to discharge to each other and the community those duties which the community, by its laws, holds incumbent on persons whose association is founded on the distinction of sex." Accordingly, by English law, and in Australia, only those marriages are recognised which preclude either party from marrying another during the continuance of the union. Thus, a marriage in accordance with the local rites in a country where polygamy is recognised and allowed would not be considered valid in Australia.

In Australia—though not till 1907 in England—marriage with a deceased wife's sister is permitted. The converse, however, does not hold good; a woman may not marry her deceased husband's brother. In Victoria it has also been held that a marriage between a man and the daughter of his deceased wife's sister is voidable—that is, it may be set aside during the lifetime of both parties; but after the death of either party the validity of the marriage, or the legitimacy of the offspring thereof, could not be questioned.

"Marriage is governed as to its *essentials*," says Mr. Foote, a well-known authority on International Law, "by the law of the domicile of the parties; as to its *forms*, by the law of the place of celebration. The law of the domicile of the parties is the proper law to decide whether the marriage can, by the use of any forms, ceremonies, or preliminaries, be effected. The law of the place of celebration is the proper law to decide what forms, ceremonies, or preliminaries shall be employed."

Accordingly, a marriage between two domiciled Australians, absolutely forbidden by English law to marry, would be invalid, although celebrated according to the proper forms in a country where such a marriage was allowed. But a marriage of domiciled Australians according to the proper forms in another Christian country would be valid, although consents or other preliminaries required by Australian law were disregarded, because these would not be *essentials* to the validity of the marriage.

Various English statutes have provided for the validity of marriages of British subjects abroad. These may, as a rule, be celebrated at any British consulate, or by "marriage officers" licensed for the purpose.

Persons under twenty-one years of age may legally marry; but an action for breach of promise cannot be brought against a minor, though a minor may sue a person of full age. If a minor ratifies a promise to marry on attaining full age, he or she may be sued on its breach. The fact that a person is already married when promising to marry is no defence to an action for breach of promise, if the person to whom the promise was given was unaware of the marriage; and the fact, indeed, would probably lead the jury to give additionally heavy damages.

When two persons have lived long together as man and wife, upon the grounds of morality and decency, a presumption is created in favour of their marriage, and evidence will be required to rebut it.

After an absence of seven years, during which time no word is heard of a husband or wife, the other party to the marriage is justified, to a certain extent, in presuming that the absent one is dead. That is to say, if a man or woman marry again under these circumstances, he or she cannot be prosecuted for bigamy

if it should be proved that the person presumed to be
dead were living. But, nevertheless, the second
marriage would be void, and any children born of it
illegitimate. Wives who have been deserted sometimes marry again without having reasonable certainty
of their husbands' deaths; in such cases it is far safer
to obtain a divorce on the ground of desertion. By a
decree in divorce the marriage is annulled, and if the
deserting husband reappeared, he would be, in law,
a mere stranger.

CELEBRATION OF MARRIAGE.—The only
persons permitted by Victorian law to celebrate marriages are ministers of religion whose names are registered in the office of the Government Statist, and the
Government Statist and registrars of marriages.

Registrars are not allowed to celebrate marriages
except between the hours of eight in the morning and
four in the afternoon. Such marriage must take
place with open door, and anyone who chooses may
be present.

Marriages cannot be celebrated unless written
notice of their intended marriage shall have been
given by the parties to the Government Statist or
minister as the case may be. In the case of the
Government Statist such notice must have been
posted in his office at least three days before the
celebration of the marriage. In the case of a marriage before a minister, this notice may be dispensed
with in cases of emergency by previous permission of
any Justice of the Peace.

These provisions do not apply to Quaker or Jewish
marriages. If such marriage is valid according to
Quaker or Jewish usages it is as valid as if it complied with the above provisions.

The breach of these regulations does not invalidate
the marriage, but renders those celebrating them liable
to punishment.

Before a marriage is celebrated the parties to it are required to make a declaration before the minister, or other person officiating, stating their age and condition (whether bachelor, spinster, widower, or widow), and their belief that there is no lawful impediment to their marriage. A false declaration is punishable as perjury.

Every marriage must be celebrated in the presence of two or more witnesses of full age, and must be registered.

The certificate of marriage must be prepared in triplicate, and signed by the person officiating, the witnesses, and the parties to the marriage, one of the latter receiving one of the copies.

If either party to a marriage, not being a widow or widower, is under the age of twenty-one, the written consent of a parent or guardian to the marriage must be produced to the person officiating.

For a minister or official to celebrate the marriage of a person under twenty-one years of age knowingly, and without the necessary consent, is an offence punishable with imprisonment. To marry a person under twenty-one in such circumstances, or to induce a minister or official to celebrate the marriage, is likewise punishable.

HUSBAND'S CONTROL OVER WIFE AND CHILDREN—In modern times a husband has practically no control over his wife's actions, in so far as they do not affect his property or his children. He is not permitted to exact her obedience by force, and it will not be ordered by law. It is true that, if a wife refuse to live with him, he can bring an action for the restitution of conjugal rights; but a judgment in his favour is practically valueless. He may not shut her up in order to force her to live with him whether he has obtained a judgment or not. If, however, she leaves his house against his will, he may ask for a divorce on the ground of desertion after the absence has continued for three years; and the courts have further held that a woman's refusal to live with her husband as his wife may constitute desertion, although she remain in his house.

In the absence of an order to the contrary, a father, even though living apart from his wife, has the custody and control of his legitimate children.

In divorce cases the Court decides who is to have the custody of the children, usually giving it to the innocent party; and the Court may always order that a child shall remain in its mother's custody if it is of opinion that it will be for the benefit of the child. When making such an order, it may also provide that the father or guardian shall pay a weekly sum to the mother for the maintenance and education of the child.

The mother, and not the father, of an illegitimate child is entitled to its custody; but the Court may deprive her of it if it appears necessary for the child's benefit. The father may be ordered by the Court to contribute to the maintenance of his illegitimate child.

While a father has the custody of his children under age, the question of his right to their wages or earnings often arises. The better opinion appears to be that, as a strict matter of law, he has no right to them. A father, in the absence of special agreement, has the right to decide in what religion his children shall be brought up and instructed. On his death, directions given by his will or by deed as to their religion must be followed; but if he leave no directions, the mother may bring up the child in her own faith, unless in the lifetime of the father the child has formed distinctive religious opinions.

All applications with regard to custody of children or their religious faith must be made to a Supreme Court judge, and may be heard by a judge sitting in

Chambers. In all applications relating to the custody of children, the Court looks primarily to the welfare of the child; and if the child has definite preferences, and is of an age capable of forming opinions, will usually be guided by its wishes as far as possible. usually be guided by its wishes as far as possible. The father cannot, since 1912 by his will, deprive his wife of any share in the guardianship of their children. If he appoints no guardian, she is sole guardian. If he appoints a guardian, that guardian acts with her, and the dying mother has, for the first time in Victoria, the power to appoint someone to be guardian jointly with the father. If the two guardians differ, the Court settles their differences.

MAINTENANCE OF DESTITUTE OR DESERTED WIVES AND CHILDREN—A husband who unlawfully deserts his wife or leaves her destitute, or who deserts his children or leaves them without adequate means of support, whether the children are legitimate or illegitimate, may be summoned before a Court of Petty Sessions to show cause why he should not support his wife or children. Whether the husband or father appears or not, the Court may order the husband or father to pay such sum as it considers reasonable in the circumstances, either weekly or monthly.

It may order him to find security that he will comply with the order, and, on his failing to find security, may commit him to gaol until he does so. If he has property it may further order that sufficient of his rents may be taken, or that sufficient of his goods and chattels may be sold, to make such allowances to the wife or children as the Court may from time to time direct.

If it appear to the justices that a man intends to desert his wife or children, they may make an order against him, and require him to find surety for compliance with the order.

Where a mother claims support for an illegitimate child from a man whom she alleges to be its father, other evidence of his paternity will be required than her own oath, uncorroborated by admissions or circumstances which tend to establish it. An admission by the defendant that he was the father of a former child of the plaintiff has been held to be sufficient corroboration of her oath that he was the father of the second.

MARRIED WOMAN'S LIABILITY FOR DEBT—Since the passing of the Married Women's Property Acts, a married woman's rights and liabilities with regard to her separate property have been, in most respects, assimilated to those of an unmarried woman.

A married woman can acquire and dispose of property, can enter into contracts, and can sue and be sued upon them, and can be made insolvent. In the latter case all her property, except that which is derived under some settlement by the terms of which she is restrained from dealing with the income before it is payable, vests in the trustee in insolvency. There is still, however, an important difference between the position of a married woman and an unmarried woman or a man with regard to debts which she may incur. The debt of the man is a personal liability. If a creditor who obtains judgment against him cannot get it satisfied by execution upon his property, he may be summoned before a Court and examined as to means. The Court may make an order that he shall pay the debt at once or by instalments, and that on failing to obey the order he shall be imprisoned.

The debts of a married woman, on the other hand, are deemed to be incurred only in respect of her separate property. Property which she has at the time of incurring the debt, and which she acquires at any time before it is satisfied, may be taken in execution. A garnishee order may be served on those who owe money to her, ordering them to hand it over to a creditor who has obtained judgment against her. Every means, in fact, may be taken to gain possession of her discoverable property which could be used in the case of a man. But she is under no personal liability to pay. She cannot be examined as to her means under a fraud summons, and ordered to pay the debt under penalty of imprisonment, even though she be in receipt of a good salary, or of income from property which is not hers to dispose of. That which is in her hands or due to her at any particular time, and in the hands of another, may be taken by the creditor if he can get it; but she cannot be otherwise constrained by law to pay him.

LIABILITY OF HUSBAND ON WIFE'S CONTRACTS—Except where she acts as his agent, or where the person with whom she contracts has reasonable cause to believe she does so, a husband is not liable on contracts made by his wife.

Where the husband gives express authority to his wife to purchase goods, for instance, he is, of course, liable if the authority can be proved. In other cases authority may be presumed.

Where husband and wife are living together, the husband will be liable for the price of necessaries supplied to his wife, unless he has warned the person supplying her not to give credit; or unless she receives an allowance from her husband for necessaries, and has been forbidden to pledge his credit, in which case it has been held that notice to the tradesmen of the allowance or the prohibition are not required.

What are necessaries is a question of fact to be determined by the circumstances of the parties.

The question of the husband's liability depends in every case on whether his own conduct is such as to justify other persons in believing that his wife acts with his authority; and if on former occasions he has paid for goods ordered in a similar manner he will probably be held liable on her orders, because he has allowed it to appear that she has been acting through out with his authority. In such cases, in order to revoke the wife's agency, he should give notice to the tradesmen that she is no longer authorised to pledge his credit.

The whole question of a husband's liability for debts incurred by his wife is one of *agency*. The mere fact of marriage is immaterial, and does not confer any authority on the wife to pledge her husband's credit; but, ordinarily, the husband acquiesces in the wife acting as his *agent*, and so his liability arises.

When husband and wife are living apart, the presumption is that the wife has no authority to pledge the husband's credit; but the husband who has allowed tradesmen to suppose that she is his agent should give them notice that he will not be liable in future for her contracts. If she has been authorised to pledge his credit by ordering goods from particular tradesmen, they should be notified specially that he will be no longer responsible. An advertisement in a newspaper to this effect would be sufficient to protect him in the case of new tradesmen who have never had his implied authority to supply goods to his wife; but it might not be sufficient in the case of former tradesmen, unless, of course, it has been brought to their notice.

IMPRISONMENT OF FRAUDULENT DEBTORS.

1. ON JUDGMENT OF THE SUPREME COURT—Where any sum of money recoverable under a judgment remains unsatisfied in the whole or in part, the person entitled to recover such money may issue a summons under the Imprisonment of Fraudulent Debtors' Act, which must be served personally upon the debtor; and if the debtor appear in pursuance of the summons he may be examined on oath by any judge of the Supreme Court touching his estate and effects, and as to his means of satisfying the debt, and as to his intention to leave Victoria without paying, or to depart elsewhere within Victoria with intent to evade payment, and as to the mode in which the liability was incurred. The person obtaining the summons and any other witnesses the judge may think requisite may also be examined.

If a person so summoned

(1) Does not attend or allege a sufficient excuse for not attending;

(2) Refuse to be sworn or to disclose any of the matters above mentioned;

(3) Does not answer to the satisfaction of the judge;

(4) Or, if the person who has incurred the debt, for which judgment has been recovered, be the defendant, and it is shown that he

   (a) obtained credit from the plaintiff under false pretences, or by means of fraud, or breach of trust; or

   (b) wilfully contracted the debt without having at the time any reasonable expectation of being able to discharge it: or

(c) has made a gift or transfer of any property, or removed or concealed the same with intent to defraud his creditors or any of them; or

(d) has then, or has had since the judgment, both the *means* and *ability* to pay the amount of the judgment, either altogether or by any instalments which the Court in which the judgment was obtained may have ordered, and has refused or neglected to pay; or

(e) that such person is about to leave Victoria without paying the amount still owing; or

(f) is about to depart elsewhere within Victoria with intent to evade payment, then the judge, if he shall think fit, may make an order that unless such person pay into Court either forthwith, or within the time limited in the order, the amount owing, together with the costs of the summons and examination, he shall be committed to prison for any time not exceeding *six months*.

A judgment debtor or defendant aggrieved by any order of commitment may, subject to such terms and conditions, and entering into such recognisance as the judge shall think fit, appeal against such order to the Full Court.

The examination must be taken down in writing, and a copy may be used on the hearing of any appeal from any order of commitment.

Any person imprisoned under an order of commitment may be discharged on payment of the amount mentioned in the order. Any judge of the Supreme Court at any time, if under the special circumstances of the case he shall think fit to do so, may direct the discharge of any person imprisoned. Imprisonment does not operate as a satisfaction or discharge of the amount due on any judgment, which may be still recovered by subsequent proceedings.

2. ON JUDGMENT OF THE COUNTY COURT—When any sum of money recoverable under a judgment of the County Court remains unsatisfied, the debtor may be summoned and examined before a judge of the County Court in a similar manner. If a party so summoned

(1) Does not attend or allege a sufficient cause for not attending;

(2) Refuse to be sworn or disclose any of the matters about which he is examined;

(3) Does not answer to the satisfaction of the judge;

(4) Or, if it appear by oral testimony or affidavit, or by both, that

(a) such party contracted the liability by fraud or breach of trust; or

(b) has made a gift or transfer of any property; or

(c) has charged, removed, or concealed the same with intent to defraud the person entitled to the money recovered, or with intent to defeat any execution issued upon the judgment; or

(5) If on the evidence the Court is satisfied that

(a) the party summoned has then, or has had since the judgment, both the *means* and *ability* to pay the amount recovered against him, or any instalments when an order to pay by instalments has been made; or

(b) that he is about to leave Victoria without paying the amount still owing; or

(c) to depart elsewhere within Victoria with intent to evade payment;

then the Court, if the judge shall think fit, may make an order that, unless such party pay into Court either forthwith or by such instalments as the judge may fix, or within the time limited in the order, the money so unsatisfied, with interest at such rate as the judge may direct not exceeding five per cent. per annum, and the costs of any fruitless writs of execution, and of the summons and examination, he shall be committed to prison for a period not exceeding *four months.*

Similar provisions to those already referred to in the case of an order of commitment in the Supreme Court exist in the County Court as to the release of the debtor upon payment, and the power of the judge to direct his discharge under special circumstances.

3. ON ORDER OF THE COURT OF PETTY SESSIONS—An order made by a Court of Petty Sessions for the payment of a civil debt, recoverable summarily, or of any instalment thereof, with or without costs, or for the payment of damages for an assault, or for trespass by cattle, or of any instalment thereof, with or without costs, or for the payment of any costs only, whether ordered to be paid by the informant or defendant, or for the value of goods detained without just cause after due notice, where an order has been made for the value of such goods unless they were delivered up, shall not, in default of distress or otherwise, be enforced by imprisonment,

(1) Unless it be proved to the satisfaction of the Court of Petty Sessions that the person, if a defendant, incurring the liability

  (a) has obtained credit from the complainant under false pretences, or by means of fraud or breach of trust; or

  (b) has wilfully contracted the liability without having at the time any reasonable expectation of being able to discharge it; or

  (c) has made any gift or transfer of any property; or

  (d) has charged, removed, or concealed the same with intent to defraud his creditors or any of them; or

(2) Unless it be proved to the satisfaction of the Court that the person making default has or has had since the date of the order the *means to pay*, and *has refused or neglected*, or refuses or neglects to pay; or

(3) Unless it be proved to the satisfaction of the Court that such person

    (a) is about to leave Victoria without paying the amount still owing; or

    (b) is about to depart elsewhere within Victoria with intent to evade payment; or

(4) Unless it be proved to the satisfaction of the Court that the person making default has neglected or refused to comply with any order under the *Justices Act* for the delivery of goods detained without due cause after due notice, and has not paid the value thereof to the party aggrieved.

The person making default may be summoned under the *Imprisonment of Fraudulent Debtors Act,* and examined before the Court of Petty Sessions. The Court, if it think fit, may make an order that unless the person making default shall pay to the clerk of Petty Sessions either forthwith, or within the time or times limited in the order, the amount owing, either in one sum or in such instalments as may be ordered, together with such costs of the summons and examination as shall be directed in the order, he shall be committed to prison for any time not exceeding *two months,* provided that no order of commitment shall be made against anyone whose estate has been sequestrated since the date of the order under which the money was recoverable.

Similar provisions to those already enumerated in the case of an order of commitment in the Supreme Court exist in the Court of Petty Sessions as to the release of the debtor upon payment, and the power of the Court of Petty Sessions by order under the hands of any two justices to direct the discharge of any person imprisoned, if under the special circumstances of the case they shall think fit to do so.

An order for commitment under these provisions
of the *Imprisonment of Fraudulent Debtors Act*
cannot be made by justices against a married woman.

Generally, creditors who have recovered judgments
should bear in mind that the provisions of the *Imprisonment of Fraudulent Debtors Act* are penal, and they
must prove their case strictly before an order will be
made. "The Act is not intended to be used as a
means of making debtors pay their debts," said the
late Chief Justice Higinbotham; "and if creditors
abuse a fraud summons for the purpose of recovering
payment, they must specifically prove the charges they
make." The order made in every case must specify
the offence; and an order will not be made against a
debtor by his consent without examination.

INSOLVENCY.

When the control of a person's estate is taken out of his hands it is said to be sequestrated.

Sequestration of a person's estate may be either voluntary or compulsory.

VOLUNTARY SEQUESTRATION—When a person is unable to pay his debts, and desires to surrender his estate for the benefit of his creditors, he may present a petition to that effect to the Court of Insolvency. A judge or chief clerk of the court may then place the estate under sequestration in the hands of one of the assignees, who are persons appointed by the Governor-in-Council under the Insolvency Acts. The petition must be accompanied by a declaration, stating that the petitioner is unable to pay his debts, and by an affidavit verifying the petition, and showing when he became unable to pay his debts as they became due. In a schedule separate lists are made out of particulars of the debts owing to secured and unsecured creditors ; of all debts due to the insolvent, and certain other matters required by the rules under the Insolvency Act 1890.

The right to petition is not given to infants or lunatics, nor to an uncertificated insolvent, who has no estate to surrender in the contemplation of the law. Married women are now subject to all the provisions, and entitled to all the benefits and disabilities of the insolvency law ; but the High Court of Australia has recently decided that the income of a married woman which is subject to a " restraint on anticipation "— that is, which she is not allowed to dispose of before receiving it—is not divisible among her creditors upon her insolvency. Executors and administrators of deceased estates may voluntarily sequestrate them :

and the greater number of partners in a firm who
are at the time in Victoria may surrender the estate
of the firm.

COMPULSORY SEQUESTRATION — If a
debtor commit an act of insolvency, a creditor or
creditors to whom debts in the aggregate amounting
to £50 are due may present a petition to a judge
either of the Supreme or the Insolvency Court. The
materials upon which the petition is based are set
out on affidavit, and the judge, if satisfied, makes an
order *nisi*. The effect of this is at once to place the
estate under sequestration in the hands of one of the
assignees. This order names a time and place where
the debtor is to appear, if he wishes to oppose the
order being made *absolute*—that is, the final adjudication of insolvency. The debtor, if he relies on any
objections other than technical defects which appear
on the face of the order itself, must file a notice of
objections within four days after the service upon
him of the order *nisi*, unless he obtains an extension
of time for filing the objections from a judge of the
Supreme Court.

On the day appointed for hearing, if the debtor
does not appear, the order is made absolute on an
affidavit showing that he has been duly served with
the order *nisi*. If he appears and opposes, the matter
is tried in the ordinary way, and the judge either
makes the order absolute, or discharges the order *nisi*
—that is, either he finally makes the debtor insolvent,
or dismisses the insolvency proceedings brought
against him.

If an unfounded or malicious petition is presented,
the court may award damages not exceeding £250;
and the respondent may also bring an action for the
injury sustained.

The death of a debtor does not affect insolvency
proceedings relating to him, unless the court otherwise order.

ACTS OF INSOLVENCY—These are set forth in section 37 of the Insolvency Act 1890, and include making an assignment to trustees for the benefit of creditors; making conveyances or gifts, or departing from the home or from the State, with intent to defeat or delay creditors; giving any preference to a creditor which, if the estate were sequestrated, would be a fraudulent preference; and failing to satisfy in whole or in part execution issued upon a judgment recovered by the petitioning creditor after having been called upon to do so.

PETITIONING CREDITORS' DEBT—The sum or sums of £50 owing by the debtor, whereby a creditor or creditors are empowered to instigate proceedings for sequestrating his estate, must be a liquidated amount—that is, it must not be for some unascertained amount or something payable upon a contingency. It need not, however, be payable immediately, if the date at which it is payable is some certain future time. Creditors upon bills of exchange can therefore petition against a debtor who has committed an act of insolvency.

If the debt be secured, the petitioning creditor is required to value his security, unless he is willing to abandon his security for the benefit of all the creditors. If he intends to retain his security, he will only be considered as a creditor, for the purpose of presenting a petition, in respect of the difference between the amount of his debt, and the amount at which he has valued the security held by him.

EFFECT OF ORDER FOR SEQUESTRA-TION—The effect of an order placing an estate under sequestration is to vest the insolvent's property absolutely in the assignee or trustee.

No sale can take place under any judgment or process for £50 or upwards until after eight days from the seizure by the sheriff or bailiff, who must also retain the proceeds of the sale for four days. If

sequestration of the debtor's estate occurs meanwhile,
the proceeds of the sale are to be paid to the assignee
or trustee; while, if the sale has not taken place,
further execution under the judgment is stayed. No
action can be brought against the insolvent for a debt
provable in insolvency, and upon the order for
sequestration being made, all proceedings in any
action then pending are stayed. The creditor
whose action is stayed can prove for his debt,
together with his costs, up to the time of sequestration
against the insolvent's estate. Actions for wrongs
committed by the insolvent or to recover damages
uncertain in amount, are only stayed to enable the
plaintiff to summon the assignee or trustee to come
in and defend the action. Having done this, the
creditor may proceed to obtain the judgment of the
court; and the judgment, when recovered, with the
costs, becomes a debt provable against the estate.
It has been held that suits in equity, such as an action
against a trustee for accounts, are not stayed by insolvency proceedings.

Actions brought by the debtor are stayed until the
assignee or trustee elects to prosecute or discontinue
them, which he must do within six weeks after notice
from the defendant in any such action. If he do
not elect to continue, he will be deemed to have abandoned the action. An insolvent may continue in his
own name and for his own benefit any action commenced by him before sequestration for any personal
injury or wrong done to himself or to any of his
family. The reason of this is that the cause of such
an action, and the proceeds of it, are outside
the insolvent's business altogether, and so do not
affect his creditors. The relief sought is monetary
compensation for a personal injury. Even an action
arising partly in respect of injury to property may
be continued by an insolvent, if the essential griev-
ance be the personal injury or insult to the insolvent
himself.

AVOIDANCE OF CERTAIN TRANSAC-
TIONS—Every conveyance, gift, or transfer of property which would amount to an act of insolvency
previously referred to is void against the assignee or
trustee. Among these acts of insolvency is any conveyance with intent to defeat or delay creditors. An
old statute in the reign of Elizabeth rendered such
conveyances void as against creditors; they are void
also against an assignee or trustee in insolvency. If
the conveyance or transfer of the debtor's property
has the effect of taking from the debtor the means of
paying his creditors or continuing his business, it is
void. Where there has been a conveyance or assignment of all the debtor's property for the benefit of his
creditors, all dealings by the trustee of this assignment will be valid and unaffected by the subsequent
insolvency of the debtor, unless the trustee had notice
at the time of such dealings that proceedings were
about to be taken to sequestrate the debtor's estate.

Secrecy in the transaction, and a transfer for quite
inadequate consideration, are certain indications of
an intent to defeat creditors.

AVOIDANCE OF SETTLEMENTS — Every
settlement of property on the wife or children, or
both, of the settlor, made after the commencement of
the Act of 1897 (unless it is made in consideration of
marriage, or is a settlement of property accrued to the
settlor in right of his wife after marriage), is void
against the assignee or trustee in insolvency unless it
is in writing, and registered in the manner and at the
times provided by the Act. If made within 12 months
of the insolvency, such a settlement is void unless it
is registered within 7 clear days of its execution in Victoria; or, if it has been executed out of Victoria,
within 21 days after the time it would have arrived
in Victoria by ordinary course of post, when posted
one week after its execution. If the settlement has
been made more than twelve months before insol-

vency, it must have been registered at least twelve months before the insolvency, or else it will be void.

Settlement is defined as any conveyance or transfer of property.

Any settlement not made before and in consideration of marriage, or bona-fidê in pursuance of a contract made before marriage, or made in favour of a purchaser or mortgagee in good faith and for valuable consideration, or being a settlement made on or for the wife or children of property, which has accrued in right of his wife after marriage, is void as against the assignee or trustee in insolvency if the settlor becomes insolvent within two years. If the settlor becomes insolvent within five years, any settlement not within the exceptions above-mentioned is likewise void, unless the parties claiming under it can prove that the settlor was, at the time of making the settlement, able to pay all his debts without the aid of the property comprised in it.

Any covenant or contract made in consideration of marriage for the future settlement on wife or children of property, not derived from the wife, or in which the settlor had not, at the date of the marriage, any interest, is void against the assignee or trustee in insolvency, unless such property has been actually transferred before insolvency.

AVOIDANCE OF FRAUDULENT PREFERENCES—Every conveyance or transfer of property, or charge thereon made, every obligation incurred, and judicial proceeding taken by any person unable to pay his debts as they become due, in favour of any creditor, with a view of giving him a preference over other creditors, is void as against the assignee or trustee in insolvency if the debtor becomes insolvent within three months. Pressure by a creditor is not sufficient to exempt the transaction from being a fraudulent preference if that creditor is paid to the detriment of others : but the provision does not affect the rights of bona-fidê purchasers and mortgagees who have given valuable consideration.

It is necessary, in order to set aside the convey-ances or transfers above mentioned, that there should be an intention on the part of the insolvent to prefer a particular creditor. A creditor actually preferred, but acting in good faith, and ignorant of the debtor's insolvent condition, would not be liable to refund to the assignee or trustee.

Payments made to the insolvent in good faith, and for value, and payment or delivery of money or goods belonging to the insolvent, as well as any contract for valuable consideration, before the date of the order of sequestration, are not rendered invalid.

PROPERTY DIVISIBLE AMONG CREDI-TORS—Property held on trust for any person by the insolvent, and the tools of his trade, together with the necessary wearing apparel of himself and family, to an amount not exceeding twenty pounds, are not divisible among his creditors. Practically everything else is so divisible, including goods in the possession of the insolvent by the consent of the real owner, if the insolvent is the reputed owner of them, or has undertaken their sale as owner.

Actual debts owing to the insolvent are included among such " goods ;" but the property comprised in a duly registered bill of sale is not, notwithstanding that the insolvent may be the reputed owner. The reason of this is that the registration of bills of sale is public, and everyone, on payment of one shilling, can inspect the register of them in the Registrar-General's office.

ASSIGNEES AND TRUSTEES—Assignees are appointed by the Governor-in-Council, and are required to give security. Their duty is to preserve the estate until the appointment of a trustee.

With the sanction of a judge, or the creditors at a meeting, the assignee may realise and take proceedings to recover any part of the insolvent estate. If no trustee is appointed, the rights and duties of the assignee are similar to those of a trustee.

A person desiring to act as a trustee in insolvency must also give security and obtain registration, which is done by a motion to the Insolvency Court. A person not registered generally as a trustee may be appointed trustee of a particular estate and may then be registered in respect of that estate upon giving the security directed by the court. After sequestration, the chief clerk of the Insolvency Court causes a notice of a general meeting of creditors to be published in the *Government Gazette*. At this meeting the creditors may appoint some fit person or persons, not exceeding two, to fill the office of trustee, at such remuneration as they from time to time determine. They may also appoint other persons, not exceeding five, to form a committee of inspection to superintend the administration of the property by the trustee. This appointment must be made by a majority in number and value of the creditors at the meeting.

For his management of the estate in the meanwhile the assignee is entitled to receive from the trustee his costs and expenses, as allowed by the court, together with the sum of five pounds when the gross assets do not exceed £200, and ten pounds when they do. If no trustee is appointed, the assignee receives such remuneration as the creditors at a meeting decide; or, if there has not been any such meeting, such amount, not exceeding 5 per cent. on the gross assets, as the court may think fit.

The trustee proceeds to realise the estate and distribute it. In carrying out these duties it is necessary for him to receive and decide upon proofs of debt from those who claim to be creditors of the insolvent.

The method of proving a debt is set forth in rules made under the Insolvency Act. Where a proof of debt is rejected by the trustee, the creditor has a right of appeal to the Insolvency Court. When rejecting a proof, the trustee must state in writing the grounds upon which he has rejected it.

The trustee has an important right of disclaimer of onerous contracts and property. Where any part of the insolvent estate consists of land burdened with onerous covenants, of unprofitable contracts, of unmarketable shares, or any other property that is unsaleable, because it binds its possessor to do some act, or pay some money, the trustee, even although he has taken possession and endeavoured to sell it, may, by writing, disclaim such property. If the property disclaimed be a contract it will be deemed to have been determined at the date of sequestration; if a lease, to have been surrendered; and if shares, to have been forfeited at the same date. Any person interested in the disclaimed property may apply to the court for possession to be given to him. Any person injured by the exercise of this privilege of disclaimer is entitled to prove as a credi-tor against the insolvent's estate to the extent of such injury.

The trustee will not be allowed to disclaim any property where an application in writing has been made to him by the person interested in the property, requiring him to decide whether he will disclaim or not, and he has not, within twenty-eight days. or such further time as the court may allow, given notice that he has disclaimed the property in question.

DUTIES OF THE INSOLVENT—The insolvent must keep the trustee informed of his changes of residence and mode of living, and is required to aid, to the best of his ability, in the realisation of his property and its distribution among his creditors. He is required to produce a statement of his affairs, list of debtors and creditors, and inventory of his property. He may be examined by the trustee and also in the Insolvency Court in respect of his property and dealings therewith. The object of this examination is to afford information to the trustee as to the insolvent's dealings with his estate; and the ordinary rules of evidence do not apply to it, as the examination is not directed to any particular issue. Any question that may throw light on the matter is, as a rule, allowed.

If the insolvent does not disclose fully all property, and deliver all that he is required by law to give up, or omits anything material in his statement, or does many other acts of fraud or concealment enumerated in the Act, he commits offences, for which he may be punished by varying sentences, according to the nature and gravity of the particular wrongdoing..

COMPOSITION, LIQUIDATION BY AR-RANGEMENT, DEEDS OF ARRANGEMENT— These are various methods of arrangement between a person unable to pay his debts and his creditors.

The creditors of a debtor may, without any proceedings in insolvency, resolve that a composition shall be accepted in satisfaction of the debts due to them. This course must be agreed to by an extraordinary resolution, which is one passed by three-fourths in number and value of the creditors, with certain formalities set forth in detail in the Insolvency Act 1890.

Liquidation by arrangement is not often resorted to in Victoria; the procedure is very similar to that of insolvency. As in the case of composition, the Act and rules provide an elaborate procedure.

Deeds of arrangement are regulated by the Act of 1897, and must be registered at the office of the Registrar-General within the time specified in the Act. These methods bind only the parties to the proceedings.

RELEASE OF INSOLVENT'S ESTATE—If an insolvent pay in full all his creditors or obtain a legal release of the debts due by the insolvent, he may apply for an order releasing his estate from sequestration. Any order of the court releasing the estate from sequestration has the effect of re-vesting the property that has not been disposed of in the insolvent. The trustee, within four days of the application, must file a report on the matter, and the court will not make any order unless satisfied that provision for the costs incidental to the insolvency has been made. If it is not proved that a dividend of seven shillings in the pound has been or will be paid to the creditors, the court will not order a release unless the insolvent show that the failure to pay seven shillings in the pound arose from circumstances for which he should not be held responsible.

CERTIFICATE OF DISCHARGE—After the expiration of three months from the date of the order of sequestration, the insolvent may give notice, by inserting an advertisement in the *Government Gazette*, that he intends to apply on a day named therein, not less than twenty, nor more than thirty, days from that date for a certificate of discharge. He must also give twenty days' notice in writing to the assignee or trustee and to every creditor by prepaid letter. The trustee or any creditor may oppose the application on giving notice of the opposition and grounds thereof. The court then considers the depositions of the insolvent and any evidence produced by him; and if there is opposition, the depositions, and any other evidence produced by the trustee or creditor: It then either grants or refuses the certificate, or grants it subject to some condition. The provision already mentioned in obtaining a release applies, and a certificate of discharge is not granted without payment of seven shillings in the pound, unless the court sees fit to dispense with this condition. Where an estate has not paid this dividend, and will not, the insolvent, at the time of obtaining the appointment for hearing his application, must set out the true circumstances on affidavit, and give not less than twenty-one days' notice to the trustee, to the official accountant, and to every creditor that he intends to apply for dispensation from the payment of seven shillings in the pound.

In actual practice certificates of discharge are granted after payment of much less than the statutory dividend of seven shillings, and frequently without payment of anything. The court must be satisfied that the failure to pay is due to the misfortune, and not to the fault, of the insolvent. The court has before it the trustee's report of the insolvent's conduct, which is made with the object of informing the court of all necessary facts. The burden of proof is on the insolvent to show his financial history, and how the losses occurred that have prevented him making the statutory payment.

For certain offences, specified in the Act, the court may refuse or suspend the issue of a certificate for a period not exceeding two years, and may also sentence the insolvent to imprisonment for a period not exceeding six months. Even though he has not been guilty of any of the offences, the court may suspend the certificate for a period not exceeding one year if the insolvent's conduct has been fraudulent or culpably negligent.

If an insolvent, before he obtains his certificate, becomes entitled to any property, the trustee, by the direction of a general meeting of creditors or the committee of inspection, may apply to the court upon notice to the insolvent, and to any other persons the court may direct, for an order to have the property dealt with, and applied for payment of the creditors. The court, in making any order, has regard to the rights of creditors whose debts have been incurred since sequestration.

EFFECT OF CERTIFICATE—The certificate of discharge absolves the insolvent from all debts provable under the insolvency. He may always bring such certificate forward as an answer to any claim made upon him afterwards for a debt of this nature.

The certificate does not release him, however, from any debt or liability incurred or remitted by means of fraud or fraudulent breach of trust, to which he was a party. Nor will it discharge him from any liability under a judgment against him in an action for seduction, or under an affiliation or maintenance order, or a judgment against him as respondent or co-respondent in a divorce suit, except to such extent as the court may order. The certificate also leaves unaffected any claims against the insolvent which would not have been debts provable under the insolvency, such as, e.g., actions for damages for personal injury.

With these exceptions, the certificate of discharge is a bar to any action unless the person who has obtained it renew his liability by a subsequent promise to pay the old debt for a good new consideration. Where a discharged insolvent could not obtain credit, and promised a butcher that if he would supply him with meat on credit he would not only pay for it eventually, but also for the meat previously supplied, it was held that this was a valid contract, being a distinct promise made on good and valuable consideration.

The certificate (discharge does not release any person who was a partner with the insolvent at the time of the insolvency, or was then jointly bound, or had made any joint contract with him.

This provision prevents the operation of the ordinary rule that the discharge of one of several persons, who are liable on a joint undertaking, discharges the others.

An uncertificated insolvent is disqualified from acting in the Legislature, in municipal bodies, or as a Justice of the Peace, as a Commissioner of the Harbour Trust, or Melbourne and Metropolitan Board of Works, or, subject to reinstatement, as an officer of the Public Service.

JOINT TENANCY AND TENANCY-IN-COMMON.

Real and personal property may be held by two or more persons, either as joint-tenants or tenants-in-common. Joint-tenants have one estate in the whole, and none in any particular part. The feature that most clearly distinguishes a joint-tenancy from a tenancy-in-common is the " Jus accrescendi," or right of accretion—that is to say, if one joint-tenant dies, the whole estate goes to the survivor. In a tenancy-in-common the shares are specified " in equal shares " " in the proportion of one-third to A and two-thirds to B," and so on. Joint-tenants have an equal, undivided interest in the whole; tenants-in-common have a distinct and several title to their shares, which are not necessarily equal. A tenant-in-common is, as to his own undivided share, exactly in the position of the owner of an entire and distinct estate. A joint-tenancy is said to be marked by unity of possession, unity of interest, unity of title, and unity of the time of commencement of the title. Tenants-in-common have only unity of possession. Trustees are invariably made joint-tenants; on the death of one, the whole estate vests in the survivor. Except in the case of trustees, as to whom there are special provisions, one of two or more joint-tenants may at any time during his life sever the tenancy, for he has an absolute power to dispose of his share, and by doing so the joint-tenancy is destroyed. Thus, if there were four joint-tenants, one could in his lifetime dispose of his undivided fourth share; but if he died without so doing the whole estate would belong to the others, each of whom could then dispose of an undivided third share, and so on. Where any doubt exists as to the nature of the estate, the Courts are strongly

inclined to favour the view that the intention would
be to create a tenancy-in-common rather than a joint-
tenancy.

By the *Partition Act* the Court is empowered to
order a sale of the property instead of a partition,
where, under the cicumstances, it appears that a sale
and distribution of the proceeds would be more beneficial to the parties interested. If the parties interested, individually or collectively, to the extent of one
moiety or upwards, request a sale, the Court, unless
good reason is shown to the contrary, must direct a
sale; and if *any* party interested request a sale, the
Court *may* direct it, unless the other parties, or some
of them, undertake to purchase the share of the party
who wishes for the sale.

JURIES.

Every householder rated at not less than twenty pounds annually who has attained the age of twenty-one years, and is either a natural-born or naturalised subject, or, if an alien, has been domiciled in Victoria for ten years, is liable, unless he comes within one of the excepted classes hereafter mentioned, to serve as a common juror. Special jurors must be natural-born or naturalised subjects, who are rated at not less than sixty pounds annually, and have, in their own names, or in trust for them, real estate of at least twelve hundred pounds, or yielding a yearly income of not less than sixty pounds.

EXEMPTIONS AND DISQUALIFICATIONS —Army officers on full pay, attorneys and solicitors and their clerks, managers and tellers of banks, barristers and their clerks, blind persons, clergymen, and schoolmasters, coroners, municipal officers, deaf and dumb persons, dentists, the Governor, members and officers of Parliament, and in the service of the Government, masters of vessels, lunatics, medical practitioners, mining managers, officers in the navy, editors, publishers, and reporters of newspapers, notaries, chemists, and pilots, are exempted from serving as jurors. Justices of the Peace are also exempted if and whenever they please. On proof, either on oath or by affidavit, to the satisfaction of the judge of any court, before which any person is summoned as a juror, that such person ought to be excused by reason of some matter of urgency, the judge may discharge him from attendance.

Every man over sixty years is exempt from serving as a juror if he claim such exemption at the annual revision of the lists. Special courts of petty sessions are held annually, in the first week of April, for the revision of the jury lists. Notice of these courts is duly given. Before the second Sunday in March in each year a notice is affixed to the door of every court of petty sessions, and post-office, and municipal hall; this states that a jury list has been made out and where it may be inspected. Every ground upon which a juror wishes to be exempted from service, except illness, must be claimed at these revision courts.

No one attainted of treason or convicted of felony, or infamous crime, unless he have obtained a free pardon, nor an uncertificated bankrupt or insolvent, nor any person unable to read and write, is qualified to serve.

The judge or chairman of any court, on proof to his satisfaction that two or more partners or clerks employed in the same establishment have been summoned for the same days, may exempt one during part or the whole of the time.

No exemption or want of qualification, if not raised before the juror is sworn, can be advanced afterwards as a sufficient reason for impeaching any verdict.

COMMON AND SPECIAL JURORS—Jury districts are constituted throughout Victoria. Before the first day of June next after receiving the lists made out at the annual revision, the sheriff causes the preparation of a " Common Juror's Book," and " Special Juror's Book " in alphabetical order. Criminal cases must be determined by a jury of twelve. As a rule, these are taken from the common juror's book; but a special jury may be ordered in the case of any indictable offence, either on the application of the Crown or of the accused. In civil cases in the Supreme Court a jury of six from the special juror's book is the ordinary jury; but a jury of twelve may be ordered on payment of the additional fees. Where, however, a party procures a trial by a jury of twelve, he is not allowed, upon taxation of costs, any further allowance than if the trial had been before a jury of six, unless the judge certifies on the record that the cause was a proper one for a special jury of twelve. On entering any cause for trial with a jury, the fees provided for the Supreme Court or County Court, as the case may be, must be paid by the party desirous of having the jury. If he is successful, of course, these fees will be allowed as part of his costs, which he will be entitled to recover from the unsuccessful party. On each subsequent day, if the trial lasts over the day, the party who demanded the jury must pay the fees. If these are not forthcoming, and the other party does not decide to pay them, the judge may conclude the case without a jury.

SELECTION OF JURORS—The sheriff, on receiving a precept to that effect from the officer of the court, appoints a time and place when he will proceed to determine the persons to be summoned as jurors. The method adopted is to place a number of parchment slips in boxes, labelled "Special Jurors" and "Common Jurors." Each slip is numbered, and, as it is drawn, the name of the juror in the juror's book to whom the number corresponds is placed upon a panel of jurors to be summoned. As soon as each panel is completed, the sheriff issues a summons to each juror. This summons must be produced when the juror subsequently applies for his fees for attendance as a juror. Upon the day upon which the persons have been summoned to appear the panel is handed by the sheriff to the officer of the court. Thereupon the officer calls aloud in court the names of the jurors.

In criminal cases the mode of striking the jury is for the officer to draw out the names of the jurymen forming the panel from a box in which these names have been deposited upon slips of paper until the proper number for the jury—twelve—has been obtained. A prisoner is permitted to challenge or object to any juror up to a specified number. For treason or a capital offence he is allowed twenty challenges; for other offences fifteen. A challenge is made by calling out " challenge " as the objectionable juror proceeds to take his seat, and before he takes it.

In civil cases the officer of the court draws the names out of the box until all the challenges are exhausted. Each party is allowed to challenge a number equal to half the number of the jury. When he has thus obtained twice the number required— that is to say, twenty-four for a jury of twelve, and twelve for a jury of six, the list is handed to the plaintiff, who is entitled to strike out six or three, as the case may be; the defendant then has a similar privilege. The remainder then constitutes the jury. If the parties do not strike out their full number, the officer of the court does so.

VARIOUS PROVISIONS—In a criminal case, where the jurors, after six hours' deliberation, are unable to agree, they may be discharged. In a civil case, after three hours' deliberation, the decision of three-fourths in a jury of twelve, or of five-sixths in a jury of six, may be taken as the verdict of all. If, after six hours, three-fourths or five-sixths are unable to agree, they may be discharged.

The card upon which is inscribed the name of any juror whose name has been called, but who has not been selected as a juryman, is returned to the box; the cards of the others are kept apart until a verdict has been given, or they have been discharged, when they are once more returned to the box.

No juror is compelled to attend for more than three consecutive business days, unless he is a juryman in a case which has not yet terminated.

Every juror summoned who has attended, whether he has actually served or not, is entiteld to compen-

sation at the rate of seven shillings a day, with one
shilling per mile per day for travelling expenses,
when the juror resides more than five miles from the
court. This mileage fee is reckoned only on one
journey; not to the court and back again. In the
event of any case occupying the court beyond three
days, for every day beyond three, and up to six, an
allowance of ten shillings per day is made; for every
day over six the allowance is one pound per day.

Jurors are allowed the use of a fire when out of
court, and reasonable refreshments. The refreshments, however, are procured at their own expense
except when they are engaged upon criminal trials
for one or more nights.

Jurors who receive a summons to attend should
be careful to do so, as they will be fined or non-
attendance. If they seek to be excused on account
of illness, or from other causes, they should have
witnesses ready to testify to the grounds upon which
they desire to be relieved of their duties.

LANDLORD AND TENANT.

The relation of landlord and tenant is created when the landlord, in consideration of a rent paid by the tenant, permits the latter to enjoy the use and occupation of his house or land.

When the property is let for a term of certain years, the tenant is a tenant for years.

A tenant from year to year, or yearly tenant, is one who, with the consent of the landlord, enters into occupation, and pays an annual rent, or a rent defined in reference to a year. This tenancy cannot be terminated, unless by consent or agreement, except by six months' notice expiring at the time of the year at which the tenancy began.

Tenancies for shorter periods are created by express or implied agreement, according as the tenant pays a half-yearly, quarterly, monthly, or weekly rent.

TERMINATION OF TENANCY — In the absence of a stipulation between the parties, or local custom, the law requires reasonable notice to be given, in order to terminate the tenancy by either landlord or tenant. What is reasonable notice has been fixed in the case of a yearly tenancy. In a quarterly tenancy, a full quarter's notice seems necessary; but in monthly and weekly tenancies, a month's or a week's notice is sufficient. It is doubtful if less than month's or a week's notice respectively would not be a reasonable notice; but it is better to err on the safe side. It must be remembered, however, that if the rent reserved be expressed as a yearly rent, the tenancy will generally be from year to year, even though the rent be payable monthly or weekly, unless it is clear from the conduct of the parties that only a monthly or weekly tenancy was intended. It is always desirable, therefore, to have the length of notice by which the tenancy may be terminated definitely set out in the agreement.

TENANT AT WILL—BY SUFFERANCE— A tenancy at will is one that has no definite term, but may be put an end to at the will of the parties. It is terminated by the death of either party.

When a tenancy expires, and the tenant continues in occupation, he is known as a tenant by sufferance. The difference between a tenant at will and a tenant by sufferance is that the former is in by right; the latter holds over by wrong after his lawful title has expired. He may be ejected by the landlord without any previous demand of possession, which is necessary to terminate a tenancy at will. This species of tenancy, however, may easily be converted into a tenancy at will, or even from year to year, by the landlord accepting rent in relation to certain periods from the over-holding tenant.

By the *Landlord and Tenant Act 1890*, any lease for years or any uncertain interest not made in writing and signed by the parties or their agents authorised by writing has the effect of an estate at will only. An exception is made of leases not exceeding the term of three years from the making, provided that the rent reserved to the landlord during the term amounts to two-thirds, at least, of the full improved value of the property. These are good, though not in writing. This provision is copied from the old English Act of Charles II., known as the " Statute of Frauds."

LEASES FOR MORE THAN THREE YEARS —Where the tenancy is to last for more than three years, it is void at law unless made by deed. Although void at law, Courts of Equity would treat it as an agreement for a lease, if it is in writing and signed by the parties, and insist upon its terms being carried out in an action for specific performance. Also, if the tenant has gone into occupation of the land under a lease which is void because not made by deed, the conditions of the tenancy will be regulated, as far as possible, by the void agreement, and will expire at the end of the term mentioned in the agreement without notice. Parties, however, should be careful to make every lease which does not come within the exception as to three years, by deed, and so avoid possible recourse to law.

Land under the *Transfer of Land Act* may be leased for any term exceeding three years by signing a lease in the form in the ninth schedule to the Act; but no lease subject to a mortgage or charge is binding against the mortgagee or person entitled to the charge, unless he has consented in writing to the lease prior to its registration.

This Act makes no change in the law as to the creation of leases for three years or less, except that the instrument, to make it effectual to pass an interest in the land, should be registered. Registration is effected at the Office of Titles; and, under the Act, an instrument is inoperative until registered. If a tenant is in possession of the land, however, his interest is protected, although the lease is not registered; and an unregistered lease is valid and binding as between the parties to it. Except where the tenant is in possession, the interests of other parties can only be affected by registration. Parties to these agreements for more than three years, therefore, should be careful to have them registered. Leases of land under the Act may still be made by deed in the ordinary form, and registered. Leases for less than three years will also be registered if desired; but if the tenant is in possession, his interest is protected, and registration is unnecessary.

CONDITIONS OF TENANCY—The conditions of a tenancy are fixed by the terms of the lease, in which the landlord and tenant usually covenant respectively to do and leave undone certain things.

In the absence of any condition to the contrary, a tenant may assign or sublet to a third party; but this does not relieve him of any of his obligations to the landlord. It is usual and prudent to have clearly stipulated in the agreement the mutual rights as to subletting and assigning the lease.

Stipulations as to payment of rates should be inserted in every lease with the utmost care, since rates are always recoverable primarily from the occupier of the property.

In the absence of agreement to the contrary, the tenant may deduct all sums of money paid by him out of the rent becoming due, or may sue the owner for what he has been compelled to pay.

In the event of a house being burned down, the tenant is not relieved of his obligation to pay rent during the term of his tenancy. In most leases there is a covenant to keep the premises insured in the name of the landlord.

Unless a landlord specifically agrees to keep premises in repair, he is not bound to do so. Neither when an unfurnished house is let is any undertaking implied on the part of the landlord that it is habitable or suitable for any other purpose to which the intention may be to put it.

The letting of a furnished house, however, carries with it an undertaking that it shall be reasonably fit for the purposes of habitation; and where the lessee found the premises infested with bugs, he was held to be justified in breaking the lease. Where unfitness for habitation arises from such a cause, or from defective drains, or the presence of contagious disease, not only is the tenant justified in repudiating the tenancy, but he may recover any loss he has incurred.

The landlord of leased premises may transfer them to any other person without consent of the lessee, and the latter remains bound by the terms of his lease. A lease may be forfeited by breaches by the tenant of conditions or covenants in the lease. The right to forfeit is lost by the landlord if he accept or distrain for rent after the date of the forfeiture.

For non-payment of rent on the part of the tenant the landlord has two remedies—(1) He may bring an action to recover the rent due. (2) He may distrain —that is to say, he may take goods, cattle, or growing crops which are upon the premises without legal action, as a pledge to compel the satisfaction of his claim.

DISTRAINT—The right to distrain, which is very ancient, is generally resorted to by landlords for the recovery of rent in arrears. It may be executed personally by the landlord, or by a bailiff, duly authorised by a document called a warrant of distress, furnished to him by the landlord or his proper agent. The person making the distress is entitled to enter the premises let at any hour between daylight and dark without permission of the tenant. He may open or unlock doors to effect an entrance, but may not break any outer door or lock. After entering, he is allowed, at any time within five days after the distress, to take and remove from the premises to some convenient place, not more than three miles distant, goods sufficient, in his opinion, to provide by the proceeds of their sale an amount which will cover the rent owing and the costs of the distress. Instead of immediately removing the goods, he may leave a man in possession on the premises. He must make an inventory of the goods taken, and serve it on the tenant, together with a notice of the distress and of the rent and charges owing. At any time within five days from the date of seizure the tenant can " replevy " his goods—that is, regain possession of them by paying the amount which he owes. If he fails to do so within the time specified, the goods may be sold by public auction. If the proceeds of the sale leave a balance, after paying rent and charges, it is to be returned to the tenant; if they are not sufficient to meet the rent and charges, the landlord may make a second distress. If a tenant fraudulently removes his goods, in order to prevent their being distrained, he is liable to pay a penalty of twice their value to the landlord, and the landlord may at any time within thirty days distrain upon the goods at any place where he may find them, and sell or dispose of them as if they had actually been distrained upon the leased premises. If the goods have been sold bona-fidê for a valuable consideration to some person ignorant of the fraud of the tenant, the landlord may not seize them.

THINGS EXEMPTED FROM DISTRESS— The tenant is given full legal remedies against any irregularities on the part of the landlord in making the distress. The tools and implements of his trade, and the necessary wearing apparel, tables, chairs, cooking utensils, bedsteads of himself and family, to a value not exceeding twenty pounds in the whole, are exempted from distress; provided that the tenant, if required in writing, delivers peaceable possession to the landlord, and has not wilfully injured the tenement during his occupancy.

By the common law fixtures or anything permanently annexed to the premises, goods delivered to the tenant in the way of his trade, goods of a perishable nature, things in actual use, wild animals, goods in the custody of the law, money, and straying cattle, are exempt from seizure by distress. The reason generally assigned is that a distress at common law was only a pledge in the hands of the landlord, the right of sale being afterwards given by statute. Consequently, fixtures and goods of a perishable nature were exempted because they could not be restored in the same condition. Machinery that could be removed without injury to the freehold would not be exempted, though it might be attached thereto for more convenient use. Goods delivered in the way of trade were exempted for the benefit of trade; things in actual use because their seizure might lead to a breach of the peace. Wild animals were excluded because there is no legal property in them; goods in the custody of the law because it would be a breach of the law to remove them. Loose money was privileged because it would not be known again, and so could not be restored in the same condition. Consequently, the privilege would not extend to money enclosed in a sealed bag. In the case of straying cattle, they might be presumed to have wandered on to the premises, owing to neglect in repairing fences. If the cattle are there by their owner's default, or with his consent, there is no privilege. If notice be given to the owner, and he fails to remove them, they may be seized next day.

By the *Landlord and Tenant Act 1909,* it is provided that where distress is levied upon his landlord, the tenant or lodger may make and serve upon the superior landlord (*i.e.,* the landlord of the tenant's landlord), or on his bailiff, or other agent employed by him in levying the distress, a written declaration:

(1) that the tenant's landlord has no right of property or beneficial interest in the furniture, goods or chattels distrained or threatened to be distrained upon;

(2) that such furniture, goods or chattels are the property, or in the lawful possession of such tenant or lodger;

(3) that they are not goods to which the Act is expressed not to apply;

(4) that £   is due by the tenant to his landlord for rent [or that nothing is due by the tenant to his landlord for rent];

(5) that the times at which the future instalments of rent will become due are [   ];
(6) that the amounts of such future instalments are [   ];
(7) that the lodger undertakes to pay to the superior landlord any rent due or to become due till the arrears are paid off.

A person who is the tenant of neither landlord, but who lives in the house, has the same protection; but his declaration need only set out (1) (2) and (3). In his case, as well as in the case of the tenant or lodger, the declaration must be accompanied by a correct signed inventory of the goods claimed.

Any person who makes or subscribes such a declaration or inventory knowing the same to be untrue in any material particular commits wilful and corrupt perjury.

If the superior landlord persists in distraining these goods, the tenant may proceed against him in Petty Sessions for their recovery, and can also sue for damages.

When in pursuance of any undertaking as mentioned, the lodger pays any sums to the superior landlord, he can set them against the rent due to his own landlord. In any case where the tenant's landlord is in arrears in his rent, the superior landlord can, by registered letter to the tenant, state the amount of rent due, and direct the tenant to pay to the superior landlord the sums due to the tenant's landlord. The notice must have annexed to it a statutory declaration by the superior landlord verifying his statements. If this is done, the lodger must pay his rent to the superior landlord.

NOTICE TO QUIT—To determine an existing tenancy otherwise than by consent, a demand for possession is necessary in the case of a tenancy at will. Periodic tenancies. such as from year to year, or from month to month, except where, by the terms of the tenancy, the parties agree to dispense with it, are determined by a notice to quit. No particular form is necessary for a notice to quit; but it must be plain in its language, addressed to the proper person, and should properly describe the premises to which it relates.

The following would be a sufficient notice to quit:—

To Mr. X, of 50 Queen-street, Melbourne.

Sir,—I hereby give you notice to quit [or that I will quit] and deliver up possession of the premises [describing them] which I (you) hold of me (you) as tenant, on the 3rd day of January next [or at the expiration of the current year of your (my) tenancy, which shall expire next after the end of one half-year from the date of this notice, or at the end of one month from the day after the date of this notice, etc., as the case may be].

(Signed)

Dated the —— day of ——, 1906.

EJECTMENT—If a tenant refuse to give up possession at the end of his term, or after receiving notice to quit, he may be dispossessed by an action of ejectment. It is provided that in any action for recovery of land the writ may be specially indorsed with a claim for rent or mesne profits by a landlord against a tenant whose term has expired, or has been duly determined by notice to quit. The effect of this is that if the defendant appears, the plaintiff may at once ask, by a summons, for final judgment against him; and unless the defendant can show some answer to the demand, he will not be allowed to defend. If he does not appear, judgment may be signed against him, by reason of his non-appearance. If he appears, and obtains leave to defend, the action is tried in the ordinary way.

SUMMARY PROCEEDINGS—Certain special remedies are given to the landlord by means of summary proceedings before justices. Where a tenant is in arrear for six months' rent, if he deserts the premises, and does not leave sufficient goods to be distrained upon, then, although no right of re-entry be given by the lease to the landlord for non-payment of rent, any two justices may go and view the premises at the landlord's request. They then affix upon the most conspicuous part a notice, stating a day, at least fourteen days afterwards, when they will return to take a second view. If upon the second view the tenant does not pay the rent in arrear, or there shall not be a sufficient distress on the premises, the justices may put the landlord in possession, and the lease to the tenant becomes void. This order of the justices is examinable on appeal by a judge of the Supreme Court at the next circuit within the bailiwick where the premises are situated; or, if they are situated in the central bailiwick, by a judge of the Supreme Court at Melbourne.

Where a tenant holds over after the expiration of his term, or when his tenancy has ended by a legal notice to quit, or in any other way (such as forfeiture for non-payment of rent, or in some other manner specified in the agreement), the landlord may give notice that he will apply, under the *Landlord and Tenant Act 1890*, before justices to recover possession. A written notice in the form specified in the eighth schedule to this Act, signed by the landlord or his agent, is served personally upon the tenant, or may be left with some person apparently living at his residence, to whom the document must be read over and explained. If the over-holding tenant cannot be found, or admission is refused to his place of abode, the posting up of the notice on a conspicuous part of the leased premises is sufficient service.

The justices then proceed to hear the matter on the day specified in the notice, and if satisfied, may issue a warrant to a constable or peace officer commanding him within a period named on the warrant not more than thirty days afterwards to enter by force, if necessary, and restore possession to the landlord. The tenant is fully protected in any case where a warrant is wrongfully procured; and if he gives a bond to the landlord or his agent in such sum as may seem reasonable to the justices to sue the person to whom the warrant was granted, and pay the costs if unsuccessful, execution of the warrant will be stayed until such action has been tried.

Where the landlord, at the time of applying for the warrant of ejectment, had a lawful right to the premises, he will not be deemed a trespasser on account of any irregularity in the procedure; but the aggrieved party may recover any damages he has sustained in an action for such irregularity. If the damage in any such action be assessed by the jury at a sum not exceeding five shillings, the plaintiff will not be entitled to any more costs than damages, unless the judge certifies that, in his opinion, full costs should be allowed.

In Victoria important alterations, among other things in the law relating to forfeiture of leases, have been introduced by the *Conveyancing Act 1904*, No. 1953. By Section 19 a lessor cannot put an end to a lease or take steps for forfeiture on account of a breach of covenant until he has served a notice on the lessee specifying the particular branches complained of, and requiring him to remedy them if capable of remedy, and make compensation in money. This provision has been introduced for the benefit of tenants. If the lessee fails to comply with the notice within a reasonable time stated therein, the lessor may enforce his rights by action or otherwise. This section does not extend to a breach of covenants in a hotel lease whereby the licence may be endangered, or to some other covenants specially excepted in this section.

LIBEL AND SLANDER.

No rule could be framed which would define satisfactorily what words are libellous and what are not. Any defamatory statement, if written, printed, or put in some permanent form, is a libel; if it is spoken, or even made only by gesture, it is a slander. A defamatory statement is one which exposes a person to hatred, ridicule, or contempt; or causes people to avoid or think ill of him; or is calculated to injure him in his trade, profession, or calling.

Every case must, therefore, depend upon the position of the parties and the surrounding circumstances. Words that would be defamatory of one man might not be so when written or spoken of another. For example, to say of a professional man that he could not read or write would be defamatory; but such a statement would not necessarily be defamatory when applied to a labourer. The test is, are the words likely to injure the reputation of another? Everyone has the same right to be protected from an assault upon his character as from an assault upon his body. " His reputation," said Vice-Chancellor Malins, " is his property, and, if possible, more valuable than other property."

PUBLICATION—In order to constitute a libel or slander there must be a publication—that is to say, the defamatory words must be communicated to some third person. No cause of action arises otherwise, because it is obvious that no injury to reputation can be incurred. Consequently there is no publication when the defamatory words are written or spoken only to the person attacked. Such a proceeding may undoubtedly cause him great annoyance; but it cannot in any way influence the esteem in which he is held by the outside world. "You cannot publish a libel of a man to himself," said the late Lord Esher, Master of the Rolls; "if a letter is not communicated to anyone but the person to whom it is written there is no publication of it." But it has been held that there is publication if the libel be written on a post card, or contained in a telegram, because it is then necessarily communicated to others; and if the writer knew when he posted a letter containing libellous matter that it would be opened by someone other than the person to whom it was addressed, that would be evidence of publication.

LIBEL A CRIME—A libel is a crime as well as a civil wrong; a slander is a civil wrong only. The reason for the distinction is that when words are written or printed, their effect is more lasting and capable of being diffused over a wider area. A criminal proceeding is designed to punish the offender. In a civil action the injured person recovers compensation in the form of damages. No one would think, therefore, of taking criminal proceedings unless the libel is of a peculiarly gross character, or in cases of libels against a sect or class, where a breach of the peace is likely to be occasioned by the virulence of the libellous publication.

In an action for damages for libel or slander, the truth of the statements complained of, if proved, affords a complete answer; for damages cannot be recovered for injury to a reputation which does not, or should not, exist.

But in a criminal proceeding for libel, the truth of the libel is no defence, unless the defendant prove, further, that it was for the public benefit that the statements should be made. The very fact that the words are true is more likely to lead to a breach of the peace. This was expressed by the old maxim, "The greater the truth, the greater the libel." This maxim is applicable only to criminal proceedings, however, and then only when the risk of a breach of the peace by publication of the libel is not outweighed by proof that its publication was for the public good.

SPECIAL AND GENERAL DAMAGES— Another distinction is made between libel and slander. When untrue defamatory words are written, the plaintiff need not show that he has suffered any pecuniary loss. The law presumes that the natural result of a libel will be to cause injury. If he has, in fact, suffered pecuniary loss in consequence of the libel, the plaintiff may recover this as well. This is known as the special damage. In slander, however, the plaintiff must always prove that he has suffered actual pecuniary loss, or special damage, unless the words spoken (1) charge him with a criminal offence; (2) impute that he is suffering from a contagious disease of a particular kind; (3) are spoken of him in relation to his trade or business; or (4) in the case of a woman, impute unchastity or adultery. In these cases the law considers, as in the publication of a libel, that the plaintiff's reputation must necessarily suffer, and he is entitled to some compensation as " general damages." If the plaintiff has not, in fact, suffered any pecuniary loss, the amount awarded as general damages may be merely nominal, or substantial, according to the circumstances proved at the trial. Mere words of idle or vulgar abuse are not actionable; even to call a man a cheat or a rogue, unless such expressions are used in relation to a man's business, will not give the injured party a right of action in the absence of proof of any special damage resulting from their utterance.

Mr. Blake Odgers, K.C., the leading authority on this branch of the law, points out that the distinction between libel and slander is not easy to justify on any scientific principle; its origin must be sought in the legal history of England. One of the reasons given for the distinction is, as previously stated, that writing or printing is permanent; it may reappear after many years, even in other countries, and continue its mischievous course. A slander, on the other hand, only reaches its immediate hearers, who may straightway forget or disbelieve it. Another reason is that writing or printing is a deliberate act, from which a malicious intenton may be inferred on the part of the author; but a slander may be uttered under temporary provocation, or thoughtlessly.

INNUENDO—Words which appear in themselves innocent may constitute a libel or slander, if they are capable of conveying a defamatory meaning, and do so in fact. Thus, the person disparaged need not be named, if his identity is perfectly clear to the reader or hearer. Again, a harmless expression may be intended to be understood in a special sense. For example, in a case dating back to the days of Queen Elizabeth, a man was called "a healer of felons," the meaning being that he was a "concealer of felons;" and this was held actionable. When words are thus used to convey a defamatory meaning, which does not attach to them if used in ordinary signification, this special meaning is called the "innuendo." In every case the judge must decide whether the words used are capable of bearing the alleged meaning. If they are not, the plaintiff's case at once fails; if he decides that the words can bear the defamatory meaning, he must then decide, or leave it to the jury, if there is one, to decide whether they do, in fact, bear that meaning.

FAIR COMMENT—Fair comment upon a matter of public interest is not libellous. The right to such comment is not, as generally supposed, confined to the press. Nothing is more important to the community than the right of free and full discussion of public affairs; and gross exaggeration will not make the comment unfair.

The test of fair comment is, according to Lord Esher, " would any fair man, however prejudiced he may be, however exaggerated or obstinate his views, have said that which this criticism has said ?" The comment must not be published maliciously; if so, it is no longer " fair " comment.

PRIVILEGED STATEMENTS — In certain cases, though the matter is defamatory, the publication does not involve liability ; in these, the occasion is said to be privileged. Statements made in Parliament, or in the course of judicial, naval, or military, or State proceedings, and reports in a newspaper of proceedings in a court of justice, if published at the time, are *absolutely* privileged ; that is to say, no action will lie in respect of them, although they may contain untrue and malicious matter. Were this otherwise, the conduct of public business would be seriously impeded, if not rendered impossible.

Upon occasions of *qualified* privilege, no action will lie where the statement is made in good faith, and does not go beyond what is reasonably suitable for the occasion. If the defendant acted maliciously, he will still be liable ; but when the occasion is privileged it will be assumed that he did not act maliciously or in bad faith, until the contrary is proved. This *qualified* privilege exists chiefly in connection with ordinary newspaper reports, and statements made in discharge of a legal, moral, or social duty; or when there is a common interest between the writer or speaker and the person to whom the communication is made. For example, if a person engaging a servant makes enquiries as to character from his late employer, the employer's reply will be given upon a privileged occasion. If the late employer's statement is libellous and untrue, he still will not be liable to an action for libel if it has been made in good faith, because he has made the statement in pursuance of a social duty. There is a common interest between him and the person who has sought his opinion of his late servant's character. If, however, the servant can show that the untrue statements were not made in good faith, but maliciously, the communication is no longer privileged, and the employer is liable. The court decides, as a matter of law, upon all the facts of the case whether the occasion is privileged. If it is, any communication made upon that occasion is privileged, unless such communication is made maliciously.

MALICE—Malice in connection with the law of libel and slander means any corrupt motive, or personal spite or ill-will. Except on occasions which are privileged, as shown above, the intention or motive with which the defamatory words were spoken or written is not material. Everyone is presumed to know that a defamatory statement will cause injury. In the award of damages, however, proof of malice becomes very important indeed; for a jury will view very differently injury to character, caused by mere thoughtless, idle gossip, and that occasioned by deliberate design or personal hatred and enmity.

LIFE INSURANCE.

A simple life insurance policy obliges the insuring company, in return for certain amounts, called premiums, paid periodically, to pay a certain fixed amount on the death of the insured person. In most offices bonuses are added to the amount for which the life is insured, and the sum payable at death is therefore often very greatly in excess of the original amount of the policy.

Policies are of many other kinds besides those of simple life insurance, one of the commonest being that which provides for the payment of a fixed sum, either on the death of the person insured or on his attaining some age specified in the policy. The rates for such policies are naturally higher than for those which guarantee payment in the case of death only.

INDUSTRIAL POLICIES—Many offices issue what are called industrial policies, under which small payments are made to them by the person insuring weekly or monthly, usually to collectors who call for them. The expenses involved in collecting these small amounts are so heavy that the terms obtainable on an industrial policy are never nearly so liberal as those given in other branches of insurance. In fact, no person who is not well acquainted with business should ever take one of these policies without consulting someone of experience, for some of them, while giving the very smallest of advantages to the insured, are worded in such terms that the careless or uneducated are very apt to misunderstand them.

WHO MAY INSURE—A person may insure his own life or that of any other person in whose life he has an interest. For instance, a wife may insure the life of her husband, upon whom she is dependent for support; a husband may insure the life of his wife; a creditor that of his debtor. In the last case the policy remains good and will be paid on the death of the insured, even though the debt has been previously paid.

MATERIAL FACTS IN INSURANCE—When a person seeks to insure his life, he is bound to disclose to the company all material facts within his knowledge, and the same duty rests upon the persons to whom the person proposing to insure refers the company.

All questions must be answered truly, whether they be verbal or in writing; and a false answer by the insured will vitiate the policy when the question is material.

A material fact is one which, if the company were aware of it, might induce it either to refuse the issue of a policy, or to demand special terms for issuing it. Therefore, the state of health of the proposer, and facts as to his health in the past, and the existence of certain diseases in his family—all facts, indeed, from which his chance of life can reasonably be deduced, are material. So also is the fact that another office has refused to insure him, or offered to insure him as a second-class life only.

A second-class life is one which will not be insured, except on the payment of a higher premium than is asked from people of that age who are considered as possessing a first-class standard of health with regard to their expectation of life.

EXTRA RISK—It is sometimes provided that a policy shall be forfeited, or that extra premiums must be paid, if the person insured goes to certain places or changes his occupation to undertake military service or other callings dangerous to life. Therefore, before effecting the insurance, it is advisable to become thoroughly acquainted with its conditions.

A condition contained in almost all modern policies is that, if the insured commit suicide, whether sane or insane, within the period of one year and thirty days, or some other specified time after insuring, the policy shall be void, and nothing shall be paid under it. If the insured commit suicide after that period has elapsed the policy is not vitiated thereby.

LOANS ON LIFE POLICIES—When a person lends money on the security of a life insurance policy the lender should secure custody of the policy, and also see that the borrower gives notice in writing to the insurance office that the loan has been made, specifying the amount, and stating that the policy has been assigned as security. Every assignment of a policy must be by memorandum of transfer endorsed on the policy in the form in the 25th schedule to the *Companies Act* 1890. The assignment is registered by the Company, and the date of registration inserted in the memorandum of transfer. Thereafter the assignee may sue in his own name on the policy assigned. Where any policy is assigned by way of mortgage, or upon any trust, such mortgage or trust must be declared by a separate document. No notice of the mortgage or trust will be entered on the memorandum of transfer, or endorsed upon the policy. The Company will not, except as hereafter mentioned, be affected by any mortgage or trust, or bound to pay the moneys due under the policy to anyone, except the insurer's representatives; or, if the policy has been assigned, to the assignee. Provided it acts in good faith, it need not concern itself further, or see to the application of any moneys payable under the policy, unless it has received express notice in writing of any trust, right, equity, or interest of any person. Where such express notice has been given, the Company would not be safe in paying over if it has any doubt as to the person entitled; and in such a case it may pay the moneys payable under the policy into the Supreme Court, which payment will be a good discharge to it. The party claiming to be entitled to the money would then be compelled to apply to the Court for payment out of the moneys, and if there was any dispute, the Court would decide.

An insurance policy is not a good security for money lent beyond what is called its " surrender value "—that is, the sum which the office would be prepared to pay to end its liability under the policy. In practically all insurance offices doing business in Australia life policies begin to acquire a surrender value after they have been running two years, and to this amount they are a first-rate security, upon which money can be borrowed on easy terms, provided a good office has insured the policy.

In some cases where the insured person cannot in the nature of things live much longer, a lender will sometimes lend more than the surrender value of the policy, since he can make the security good by paying the premiums himself if the insured fail to do so, and he knows that he will not have to pay them for any great length of time.

LIABILITY OF LIFE POLICY FOR DEBTS OF INSURED—Section 3 of the Life Assurance Companies Act of Victoria, Act No. 1679, is of very great importance in freeing life policies from liability for the debts of the insured, except in certain cases. Sub-section 3 of that section is as follows:—" Notwithstanding anything contained in his will or any codicil thereto, on the death of any person, the property and interest of such person in any policy or policies of assurance of his life, maturing only at his death, shall not be assets for the payment of his debts except those (if any) for the payment of which he shall, in such will or codicil, declare an intention to make such property and interest assets by words expressly referring to such policy or policies, and expressly negativing the provisions of this section; but if he dies within four years after the date of any policy, a portion of the sum paid under such policy, equal to the amount of premiums actually paid in respect of so much of the sum assured as exceeds one thousand pounds, shall be assets for the payment of his debts."

The effect of this section is to practically free life policies from the payment of the debts of the insured, unless he takes the most deliberate means to make them liable. Up to the sum of £1000 the immunity is absolute. Any premiums actually paid in respect of the balance for which the life is insured over £1000 may be taken on behalf of creditors, from the insurance money received, if the insurance is effected within four years of the death of the insured.

The object of this last proviso is to prevent creditors suffering loss through a debtor spending his assets in taking out a large life policy from which they can reap no benefit on his death. The law provides that the money of the debtor actually so spent shall be eventually available for creditors.

By the *Companies Act 1903*, section 4, this immunity from liability for the debts of the insured after his death is extended to policies not maturing only at his death (that is, e.g., policies maturing at a certain age or death) to the extent of £1000. Above this sum on such policies, however, the amount payable by the insurance company would be assets for the payment of his debts.

If a person who has insured his own life becomes insolvent, the policy, up to the sum of £1000, is free from liability to his creditors, unless the insolvency happens within two years of insuring. And even in this case the insolvent, or any person on his behalf, is given the right of buying back the policy, by paying to the trustee for the creditors the actual amount of the premiums spent on such policy.

MORTGAGE OF LANDS.

A mortgage is an instrument by virtue whereof land is assigned or charged as security for the repayment of a loan, with a condition that it shall be reassigned or released from the charge on the satisfaction of the debt.

Under the general law a mortgage conveyed the mortgaged property from the mortgagor to the mortgagee, the former merely retaining a right to redeem—that is, to have the property reconveyed to him on payment of the debt, which right in the land is called the "equity of redemption."

The ordinary mortgage of land, which is not under the Transfer of Land Act, still operates as a conveyance on these terms; but a mortgage of land under this Act does not transfer the title or legal estate to the mortgagee. It merely gives him the right to do certain things in order to secure repayment of the loan.

MAKING AND REGISTRATION—A mortgage of land not under the Transfer of Land Act is made by a deed under seal.

A mortgage under the Transfer of Land Act is made by an instrument—a document which is not sealed, but is of like effect. It is ordinarily registered at the Titles Office, where notice of the mortgage is entered on the title to the mortgaged property. A mortgage which is not registered is, however, binding as between the parties to it. Should there be two mortgages on one property, one registered and the other not, the registered mortgage would take precedence over the unregistered, though it were executed subsequently, and it is therefore always desirable to register.

Mortgages of land under the general law may be, and often are, registered. Registration is not necessary to their efficacy for any purpose, but it gives priority.

What is called an " equitable mortgage " is effected by a borrower depositing title deeds with a lender, which, in the absence of any written document, is held to give the lender the rights to claim the execution of a legal mortgage.

COVENANTS—When land is mortgaged the mortgagor and the mortgagee covenant with one another to do certain things, which are usually set out at length in the mortgage deed. Under the Conveyancing Act of Victoria a mortgage of land under the general law may be made as a " statutory mortgage " in a short form, and the covenants by mortgagor and mortgagee are implied by the Act. Other useful forms are given in the schedules to the Act.

An essential covenant on the mortgagee's part is to allow the mortgagor quiet possession of the mortgaged property while he is not in default with payments of principal or interest; and on the mortgagor's part to pay the principal and interest on the due dates; to repair and keep in repair buildings and improvements on the land; and to allow the mortgagee or his agents free entrance at all reasonable times to inspect the security.

In the absence of any statement to the contrary, these covenants on the part of the mortgagor are implied in all mortgages under the Transfer of Land Act. The form of mortgage given in the twelfth schedule to that Act includes also a covenant to insure against fire in the name of the mortgagee, while any other covenants can be added at the will of the parties.

Generally speaking, the effect of breach of covenants by the mortgagor is to give the mortgagee the

right to demand repayment of the money lent, and
to sell the land if he does not receive it; but there is
a special provision for relief against action taken for
failure to insure if the breach of covenant results from
accident or mistake, and not from fraud or gross
negligence, and if the mortgagor has reinsured.

MORTGAGEES' POWER OF SALE—All
mortgages, whether under the general law or
the Transfer of Land Act, give the mortgagee the
power of sale for failure to pay principal or interest
or for the breach of other covenants. Where it is
not provided in the mortgage what time must elapse
after default before the mortgagee takes action, he
may give notice of intention to sell one month after
the breach of covenant, and if all that is owing is not
paid in the meantime, may, after a month has expired
from the date of the notice, sell the land either by
public auction or private contract.

If the money realised by the sale is more than sufficient to pay the mortgagee's debt, and all costs and
expenses of sale, the balance, less this amount, is
handed over to the mortgagor.

DISTRAINT—In addition to the power of sale,
the mortgagee as a rule under covenants in the
mortgage has a right to distrain for monies
owing in the same way that a landlord may
distrain upon a defaulting tenant's goods. Further,
he may bring a legal action for recovery of anything
due to him on covenants in the mortgage, or for
damages sustained by their breach.

If distraint upon goods on the mortgaged property,
or the sale of the property, do not realise enough to
discharge the debt, the mortgagee does not lose his
right to the balance of the money owing, but may
bring an action to recover it, and, on obtaining judgment, may issue execution against other property
of the mortgagor.

FORECLOSURE—Another right possessed by the mortgagee is that of foreclosure—that is, of putting an end to the mortgage and taking the mortgaged property, if it is impossible to sell it at a price which will cover the mortgagor's indebtedness. Under the old law foreclosure did not relieve the mortgagor of his liability ; but the Conveyancing Act of Victoria makes the act of foreclosure an extinction of the debt. If a mortgagee takes absolute property in the land, he can no longer claim anything from the mortgagor in respect of the mortgage.

EXECUTOR OF MORTGAGEE—TRANSFER —The executor or administrator of a mortgagee acquires all the rights of the deceased in respect of the mortgaged property. The executor or administrator acquires all his liabilities, as far as the assets of the deceased are sufficient to satisfy them, but he is, of course, under no personal liability to meet any deficiency.

The holder of a mortgage can transfer it to any person he chooses without the permission of the mortgagor. The mortgagor, on payment of the debt when it has become due, can claim the transfer of the mortgage by the mortgagee to any person whom he may name, who then becomes mortgagee. Formerly, a debtor had only the right to have the land freed from the mortgage on repaying the money owing; but the provision above mentioned enables him to obtain a new loan in order to pay off the original mortgagee, and to transfer the security to the person who lends the money, without the expense of cancelling one mortgage and executing another.

PARTNERSHIP.

NATURE OF PARTNERSHIP—Partnership is
the relation which subsists between persons carrying
on a business in common with a view of profit. It
is sometimes difficult to determine whether a partnership is constituted or not. In determining the question, regard is had to certain rules. Joint-tenancy,
tenancy-in-common, joint property, common property, or part ownership, does not of itself create a
partnership, nor does the sharing of gross returns.
The receipt by a person of a share of the profits of a
business is *prima-faciê* evidence that he is a partner;
but the receipt of such a share or a payment contingent on or varying with the profits of a business does
not of itself make him a partner in the business. The
main rule in determining the existence of a partnership is, says Lord Lindley, " that regard must be paid
to the true contract and intention of the parties as
appearing from the whole facts of the case."

RELATIONS OF PARTNERS TO PERSONS
DEALING WITH THEM—Every partner is an
agent of the firm, and may bind the firm in doing
any act in its usual way of business; unless he has, in
fact, no authority to deal for the firm in that particular matter, and the person with whom he is dealing
either knows this, or does not know that he is a
partner. Where a partner pledges the credit of the
firm for a purpose outside its ordinary business, the
firm is not bound, unless he is authorised by the other
partners. If it is agreed between partners that some
restriction shall be placed on the power of any one
partner to bind the firm, no act done in contraven-
tion of this agreement is binding in respect of persons
who have notice of it. Every partner is liable jointly
with the others for all debts incurred while he is a

partner; and after his death his estate is liable for such debts so far as they are unsatisfied, but subject to the prior payment of his separate debts. Notice to any partner relating to the business operates as notice to the firm except in the case of a fraud on the firm committed by that partner. An admission concerning the affairs of the partnership made by any partner in the ordinary course of business is evidence against the firm.

RELATIONS OF PARTNERS AS BETWEEN THEMSELVES—As between themselves, the rights of partners are generally specified in the partnership agreement, and they may be varied by the consent of all the partners. Partnership property must be held and applied exclusively for the purposes of the partnership. In the absence of any agreement to the contrary, partners are entitled to share equally in the capital and profits of the business, and must contribute equally to losses. The firm must indemnify every partner for payments made or liabilities incurred in the proper conduct of the business or anything necessarily done for the preservation of the business or firm property. A partner making an advance for the purpose of the partnership beyond the capital he has agreed to subscribe, is entitled to interest at seven per cent. A partner is not entitled, before the ascertainment of profits, to interest on the capital subscribed by him. Every partner may take part in the management, and no partner is entitled to remuneration for so acting. No person may be introduced as a partner without the consent of all existing partners. In ordinary matters a difference may be decided by a majority; but no change in the nature of the business may be made without the consent of all. The books of the partnership are to be kept at the place of business, and every partner has a right to inspect them at any time. No majority can expel any partner unless a power has been conferred by express agreement between the partners.

Where no fixed term has been agreed on, any partner may determine the partnership by giving notice to all the others. Where a partnership for a fixed term is carried on afterwards without any new agreement the rights and duties of the partners remain the same, so far as consistent with a partnership at will; that is to say, any partner by notice may terminate the partnership, but meanwhile it is carried on under the old conditions. Every partner must account for any benefit received in connection with any partnership transaction; and if without the consent of the other partners, he carries on any business of the same nature as, and competing with, that of the firm, he must account for all profits.

An assignment by a partner of his share does not entitle the assignee to interfere in the business, but only to receive the share of profits of the assigning partner, and he must accept the account of profits agreed to by the partners; in case of a dissolution, the assignee is entitled to the share of the assets due to the assigning partner, and for the purpose of ascertaining that share to an account as from the date of dissolution.

DISSOLUTION OF PARTNERSHIP—Subject to any agreement between the partners, a partnership is dissolved

    (a) if entered into for a fixed term by the expiration of that term;

    (b) if for a single undertaking, by its termination;

    (c) if for an undefined time by notice by any partner of his intention to dissolve. In this case the partnership is dissolved as from the date mentioned in the notice; or if no date is mentioned, as from the date of the communication of the notice.

Subject to any agreement between the partners, the death or insolvency of any partner dissolves the partnership; if a partner suffer his share of the partnership property to be charged for his separate debt, the partnership may be dissolved at the option of the other partners. It is in every case dissolved by the happening of any event which makes it unlawful for the business to be carried on.

The Court may, on the application of a partner, decree a dissolution

    (a) when a partner is lunatic, or of unsound mind;

    (b) when another partner becomes permanently incapable;

    (c) when another partner has been guilty of conduct which would, in the opinion of the Court, prejudicially affect the carrying on of the business;

    (d) when another partner wilfully breaks the partnership agreement, or so conducts himself that it is not reasonably practical to carry on;

    (e) when the business can only be carried on at a loss;

    (f) whenever circumstances have arisen which, in the opinion of the Court, render it just and equitable that the partnership be dissolved.

After the dissolution the authority of each partner to bind the firm continues so far as necessary to wind up the business, and complete transactions begun and unfinished. The partnership assets must be applied in payment of the debts of the firm, and the surplus distributed between the partners. In settling accounts between partners after a dissolution, the following rules, subject to any agreement, are observed:—

    (a) Losses including losses and deficiencies of capital are paid first out of profits, next out of capital, and, lastly, if necessary, by the partners individually in the proportion in which they were entitled to share profits;

(b) The assets of the firm, including the sums (if any) contributed by the partners to make up losses, are applied—

(1) In paying the debts of the firm to outside creditors;

(2) In paying to each partner rateably what is due from the firm to him for advances, as distinguished from capital;

(3) In paying to each partner rateably what is due from the firm to him in respect of capital;

(4) The ultimate residue (if any) is divided among the partners in the proportion in which profits are divisible.

It cannot be too strongly urged upon persons entering into partnership that they should have a partnership agreement properly prepared, and should see that their intentions are clearly expressed, and that all contingencies are, so far as possible, provided for. All the details of the legislative provisions as to partnership will be found in the *Partnership Act 1891*, No. 1222; but these, so far as regards the relationship of partners between themselves, are, as a rule, only to be in force so far as any agreement does not provide to the contrary. In other words, the partners as between themselves may make any agreement they choose.

PAWNBROKERS AND PAWNING.

Before any person can enter on the business of a pawnbroker in Victoria he must obtain a licence, which costs ten pounds annually, and which will only be issued to a person producing a recommendation, signed by five householders residing in the district. This licence is revocable by a court of petty sessions on proof of the pawnbroker's dishonesty.

REDEMPTION OF PLEDGES—Any article upon which a pawnbroker lends money is termed a "pledge," as it is retained by the lender as security for the debt, until redeemed by payment of principal and interest, or forfeited by failure to redeem within the time fixed by law.

The time allowed for redemption is six months, not including the day of pawning, for any pledge other than an article of wearing apparel, and three months, not including the day of pawning, for any pledge which consists of wearing apparel.

This time may be extended by agreement made at the time of pledging or subsequently; but any agreement for forfeiture within a shorter period is absolutely null and void. Where the term is longer than that fixed by law, the fact must be entered on a pawn ticket. If a pawnbroker forfeits a pledge before the due date, he is liable to pay a penalty not exceeding £50 to the borrower.

SALE OF PLEDGES—A pledge duly forfeited may be sold. If more than 5/- has been lent on it, the sale must be by auction, of which an advertisement, with a catalogue of the articles to be sold, mentioning when each was taken in pawn, must appear twice in some Victorian newspaper, at least four days before the sale. Neither the pawnbroker nor any person on his behalf may buy at the auction.

If the sale of a pledge realises more than the amount owing on it for principal and interest, and cost of sale, the balance may be claimed by the owner or his representatives within 12 months of the date of selling.

The owner of a pawned article is deemed to be the person who presents the pawn ticket, unless there is reason to believe it has been dishonestly obtained by him. When a pawn ticket is lost, a duplicate may be issued by the pawnbroker to the person claiming to be the owner on his making a statutory declaration.

INTEREST CHARGEABLE—A limit of interest chargeable by pawnbrokers is fixed by law. The maximum rate allowed is:—

2d. per month for each 2/6 advanced up to the sum of £10.

For sums in excess of £10, a rate not exceeding 50 per cent. per annum.

If an article be redeemed in less than a month, a full month's interest may, nevertheless, be charged. If, however, it be redeemed within one week after the expiration of the first or any other month, nothing can be claimed on account of the extra days. If the pledge be redeemed within a fortnight, an extra half-month's interest will be payable; while any period exceeding a fortnight counts as a full month.

PAWN TICKETS—Every pawn ticket must be signed by the pawnbroker, and have clearly stated upon it the number of the pledge, the date at which the pledge was received, the residence and calling of pledgor, a description of the article or articles pledged, the amount lent upon them, and the rate of interest. These particulars, together with a statement as to whether the pledge has been redeemed, sold, or otherwise disposed of, must also be entered in a book in the pawnbroker's shop, and neglect to comply with these conditions renders the pawnbroker liable to a fine of any sum up to £50.

VARIOUS PROVISIONS—A pawnbroker is forbidden to deal with persons under fourteen or with drunken persons. He may not do business before eight o'clock in the morning, or after nine o'clock at night, except on Saturdays, and the days preceding Good Friday and Christmas Day, when he may keep open until 11 o'clock. He is not permitted to carry on his business on Sundays or Christmas Day or Good Friday. He must restore to the owner stolen goods which have been pawned to him, either with or without compensation, as may be ordered by a court. Where a pledger fails or refuses to give a satisfactory account of himself, or the means by which he became possessed of an article which he desires to pawn, or otherwise gives the pawnbroker good reason to suspect fraud. the latter is authorised to seize the article and the person seeking to pledge or redeem it, and to give him into custody.

The provisions relating to pawnbrokers apply also to their executors or administrators, except that no executor or administrator is liable to pay any penalty out of his own money unless it has been incurred owing to his own act or neglect.

PROBATE AND ADMINISTRATION.

In order to deal legally with the estate of a deceased person, it is generally necessary to obtain probate of his will if he has left one, or letters of administration if he has died intestate. Probate of the will is obtained by the executor, who is the person appointed by the deceased in his will or codicil. When a person dies intestate, the court appoints an administrator, generally the nearest, or one of the nearest, of kin to the deceased.

There is a considerable difference in the powers of an executor and administrator before obtaining a grant of probate or administration.

The executor, being the nominee of the deceased, may at once perform most of the duties relating to his office. He can proceed to collect the assets, pay the debts, and even bring an action in connection with any property of the deceased of which he has actually got possession. But with respect to an administrator, the general rule is that he can do nothing until letters of administration are granted to him; inasmuch as he derives his authority, not from the expressed wish of a testator, but entirely from his appointment by the court.

PAYMENTS WITHOUT PROBATE—If a depositor in any savings bank dies, leaving moneys not exceeding £100, and probate of the will, if a will has been made, or letters of administration be not produced to the trustees of the institution, they may pay, after three months, such moneys to the widow or such person as may seem to them entitled to the effects of the deceased.

Upon the death of a person whose life is insured for a sum not exceeding £200, if no probate or letters of administration be taken out within, three months, the company may pay the amount of the policy and bonuses to the widow, or widower, or next-of-kin of the deceased.

Of course, the persons in these cases to whom the money is paid only receive for their own benefit such sum as they may personally be entitled to ; they will be liable to account to the executor or administrator, if probate or administration be afterwards granted, for what they have received, and to pay over anything in excess of their own shares in the estate.

As soon as probate or administration is granted, the executor or administrator becomes, for all purposes, the legal representative of the deceased. He then can, and should, collect the debts due to the estate, take possession of the property, pay the debts properly owing, and distribute the estate among those entitled to it.

PROBATE OF SMALL ESTATES—Where the estate of a deceased person is under £500 in value, it is not necessary for the executor or administrator to engage a lawyer to obtain probate in Victoria. If he goes personally to the County Court registrar whose office is nearest to the abode of the deceased, he is entitled to obtain the aid of that officer in obtaining a grant. The registrar will fill up the necessary affidavits, advertisement, and other documents required, and forward these to the office of the Master-in-Equity. In Melbourne, the applicant can go direct to the office of the Master-in-Equity, Law Courts, William-street. When the grant of probate or administration has been made, the applicant can obtain the document containing the grant from the registrar on payment of the necessary fees and probate duty, if any duty is payable.

Where the estate is worth more than £500, the executor must either employ a solicitor or do the work personally, without assistance.

HOW THE EXECUTOR PROCEEDS—The first step necessary is to insert an advertisement once in some newspaper circulating in the State, giving a clear fortnight's notice of intention to apply for probate. After this time has elapsed the original will must be filed in the Probate Office, and, with it, affidavits from the executors, stating the date of deceased's death, the value of his assets, and the fact that he has left a will, with its date. The name and residence of each of the attesting witnesses, and of the executor or executors, must also be given, as well as a statement that no caveat has been lodged against the application up to the day upon which it is made. If the will has been made by a marksman, extra precaution is necessary, and there must be an affidavit, if possible, by one of the witnesses, stating why the testator executed the will by affixing his mark.

If everything is in order, the registrar then grants probate without anything further being done by the executor. If there is any irregularity, or anything which arouses doubt in the mind of the registrar, he refers the matter to the Supreme Court, to which the executor must apply, either personally or through a lawyer.

CAVEATS—Wherever a caveat has been lodged against an application for probate, the registrar must refer the matter to the court. The court then appoints a day for hearing the application; if the person who has lodged the caveat appears, and objects to the grant, the matter is put into the ordinary list of cases to be tried. At the trial the executor brings witnesses to prove the will, and the person who has lodged the caveat brings witnesses to prove the grounds upon which he alleges probate should not be granted: and the court then decides. If the person who has lodged the caveat does not appear, or withdraws the caveat, probate will be granted on filing an affidavit that no other caveat has been lodged.

STATEMENT OF ASSETS—GRANTING OF PROBATE—Before the actual issue of the probate document to the executor, he must file in the Probate Office a detailed statement of the assets of the deceased, in order that the estate may be assessed for duty. The debts owing by the deceased must be set out in this statement, or no deduction of duty will be allowed on their account. Probate duty is paid on the net value of the estate.

The assessor examines this statement of assets, querying anything to which he takes exception, and the matter must be finally settled and the duty paid before the probate is handed over to the executor. This is a parchment containing an exact copy of the will and a statement that probate has been granted to the executor.

Armed with this, the executor is in a position to draw the deceased's money from the bank, and to do anything necessary to collect and administer the estate. Until he has the document, banks and others holding any property of the deceased will not (with the exceptions mentioned above) hand it over to the executor, and therefore he must borrow or otherwise raise the money necessary to pay the duty before probate issues to him, afterwards, of course, repaying it from the estate.

ADMINISTRATION — NEXT-OF-KIN — If there is no will, the widow or one of the next of kin applies for administration. The person seeking administration must insert advertisements, as in the case of a person seeking probate, and file affidavits setting forth the death of the deceased, the time of death, the fact that he died intestate, leaving property in Victoria, and its value, the relatives or next-of-kin, so far as known, the character in which

the applicant is claiming to be entitled to the grant;
and also that there is no will, and no caveat has been
lodged up to the date of the application.

ADMINISTRATION BONDS—Every person to
whom a grant of administration is made must execute
a bond to the Chief Justice. The bond is in order
to ensure the due collection and distribution of the
assets of the estate, and is made subject to a penalty.

The penalty of the bond is made equal to the
amount of the property of the deceased; and two
sureties are required. The court may in any case,
however, reduce the amount of the penalty of the
bond, and dispense altogether with sureties, if it think
fit. When the estate is over £5000, a bond is not
required above that amount.

The object of these provisions is to enable persons
interested in the estate to obtain redress from the
administrator or his sureties if the condition of the
bond is broken and the estate is wasted or lost by
negligence or wrongdoing of the administrator.
This is done by applying to have the bond assigned,
and the person to whom it is so assigned may then
bring an action as trustee for all the persons interested in the estate, and recover the amount from the
administrator and his sureties.

Where the deceased has left no debts owing, or
where the person applying for administration is
entitled to the whole estate, or where all interested
in the estate consent, the court usually dispenses with
sureties. The court must be satisfied, however, that
those persons who consent thoroughly understand
that the dispensing with sureties will give the administrator uncontrolled management of the estate, and
that they will have no estate but his own to resort to
if he should act improperly.

The sureties to an administration bond are required
to "justify"—that is, satisfy the Master-in-Equity

that they possess sufficient property to enable them to recoup the estate up to the amount to which its value has been sworn, if the administrator should not fulfil the condition of his bond and properly administer the estate. When sureties cannot be obtained to justify to the whole value of the estate, they are sometimes permitted by the court to justify to a smaller amount.

Where those entitled to obtain probate or administration do not apply, a creditor of the deceased may obtain a grant of administration, after publication of advertisements and filing affidavits, setting forth the circumstances and particulars of the estate required in the case of an ordinary grant.

THE CURATOR—The curator of the estates of deceased persons is an officer whose duty it is to apply for a rule to administer the estates of deceased persons when no one else is entitled or ready to obtain probate or administration, and the estate in consequence is liable to waste or injury. The curator may also be appointed by will, in which case he is bound to apply to the court for a rule to administer the estate. The curator is not required to give a bond, as he is a public officer.

In any case where the executor named in a will does not prove it, or renounce probate, within six weeks after the testator's death, any person interested in the estate, or the curator, or any creditor, may apply for an order calling upon him either to obtain probate or show some reason why administration should not be granted to the applicant. The court, then, may make a grant of administration if the executor does not appear; and if he does, it may make any order that may seem just as to granting probate or administration and costs of the application. An executor who has not proved the will within six weeks may also be ordered to bring the will into court.

EXECUTOR'S RIGHT TO COMMISSION—
An executor or administrator is allowed a commission out of the assets of the deceased person for his work in managing the estate. This is fixed by the Supreme Court, or its chief clerk. But, where a testator specifies in the will the amount to be allowed, the Court will consider whether this amount is sufficient, and may allow more if it thinks fit. To obtain the commission, the executor or administrator should pass his accounts. This process consists in bringing before the chief clerk of the Supreme Court a detailed list of the amounts received and expended on behalf of the estate. An allowance not exceeding 5 per cent. may then be given. The usual practice is to allow 2½ per cent. on the corpus or capital, and 5 per cent. upon the net income; but the amount may be varied according to the labour involved.

TRUSTEE COMPANIES—Trustee companies, duly incorporated, may be appointed executors by will, or be authorised by the persons entitled to obtain probate or administration to apply in their stead for letters of administration. After probate or administration has been granted to a private person, it may also, with the consent of the Supreme Court, be transferred to a trustee company. These companies are not required to execute a bond, as their entire assets are liable for the proper administration of the estate; the amount of their commission for acting is fixed by the various statutes which incorporate them, and is 2½ per cent. on capital and 5 upon income, as above.

CARE REQUIRED IN ADMINISTRATION—
When applying for a grant of probate or administration, the executor or administrator is required to swear that he will collect and administer according to law the assets of the deceased; and will make a true inventory of all that has come into his posses-

sion or knowledge, and deposit this, within three months after the order granting probate or administration, in the Master-in-Equity's office; and will also file an account of his administration, showing what still remains uncollected within fifteen months. These are known respectively as the " three-months' " and " fifteen-months' " accounts.

Executors and administrators are usually very careless in respect to these accounts, and frequently neglect to file them. They should be careful to do so, as otherwise they will not be allowed commission, and they are committing a breach of trust by not doing what they have sworn to do. Someone interested in the estate might proceed against them to compel them to perform their duty. Indeed, the office of executor or administrator is not one to be lightly undertaken by persons without business experience. As a rule, it is far safer in an estate of any size, which requires skilled management, unless reliance is placed on the judgment and discretion of particular individuals, to appoint a company as executor or administrator. The estate is then in the hands of experts, whose daily business it is to deal with the estates of deceased persons, and realise them to the best advantage, but strictly in accordance with law.

The charges made for obtaining probate or administration by solicitors should not be very large, except where trouble is experienced in making out the account for duty. This may occasion considerable work, involving expert knowledge. Apart from this, however, the matter is one of routine, according to a very simple procedure.

FOREIGN PROBATES—Where probate or administration has been granted to a deceased person in some place outside Victoria, and such person has left property in the State, it is necessary to obtain a grant in Victoria in order that such property may be dealt with. This may be accomplished by the executor or administrator, or some person authorised by their power of attorney, applying to have the seal of the Supreme Court affixed to the original grant. An advertisement must be inserted that such application is about to be made, and that no caveat has been lodged up till the date of the application.

As soon as the probate or letters of administration are sealed, the executor or administrator, or his attorney-under-power, as the case may be, is deemed to be for every purpose the executor or administrator of the estate of the deceased in Victoria.

The object of these provisions is to prevent Victorian property falling into the hands of anyone but those entitled to it, though residing abroad; and also to ensure the payment of duty, as the seal will not be affixed, and the property cannot consequently be dealt with, until duty is paid.

PROMISSORY NOTES.

DEFINITION—A promissory note is an unconditional promise in writing made by one person to
another, signed by the maker, engaging to pay on
demand, or at a fixed or determinable future time,
a sum certain in money to the order of a specified
person or to bearer.

The following is the ordinary form of promissory
note, written on paper embossed with the proper
duty stamp:—

£50.

Melbourne, July 1st, 1905.

— months after date [or on demand] I promise to
pay Hans Anderson or order. [or bearer] fifty
pounds.

Payable at [usually name and place of a banker].

John Brown.

A promissory note is incomplete until it has been
delivered to the payee or the bearer.

JOINT AND SEVERAL LIABILITY—A promissory note may be made by two or more makers.
If it runs, "we promise to pay," and is signed
by both, they are liable jointly, not jointly and
severally. Though each is liable for the whole
amount, a judgment obtained against one, though
it were unsatisfied, would be a bar to action against
the other.

If the note runs, "I promise to pay," and is signed
by both, they are jointly and severally liable. Either
or both of the debtors may be sued in one action,
and a judgment against one, if unsatisfied, is no bar
to an action against the other. The debtors are left

to adjust matters as to their liability to one another between themselves.

INDORSEMENT — TRANSFER—The person who indorses a promissory note renders himself liable upon it if it is not paid by the maker; but where a promissory note, payable on demand, has been indorsed, and is not presented for payment within a reasonable time, the indorser is discharged from liability. What is a reasonable time is in each case a question of the particular facts and of the usage of trade.

When a promissory note is, in the body of it, made payable at a particular place, it must be presented there for payment to render the maker liable. In any other case presentment for payment is not necessary to render the maker liable.

The indorser, however, can never be rendered liable without presentment to the maker for payment. When a place of payment is indicated by way of memorandum only, and not in the body of the note, a presentment to the maker elsewhere, if sufficient in other respects, will suffice to render the indorser liable.

Promissory notes are transferable from one person to another, and the holder of a promissory note in due course—that is, who takes it in good faith, and for value, without notice of any defect—is not affected by any irregularity in the circumstances which led to its making, and which might, perhaps, prevent the person in whose favour it was made recovering from the maker.

If a promissory note has been presented for payment and is dishonoured, then the holder of it may sue any of those who have indorsed it.

A promissory note must be made in Victoria on Government forms with embossed stamps. A promissory note unstamped, or insufficiently stamped, is bad.

CARE NEEDED IN RENEWING—Farmers who do business with storekeepers in Victoria very frequently give promissory notes by way of payment, and, being unable to meet them at the due date, obtain a renewal, and sign another note in place of that which is not met. In such cases any person who signs a second note should be very careful before delivering it to obtain possession of the former one, or to see that it is destroyed. Though the second note is given in respect of the same debt as the first, the maker may be held liable on it, and have judgment given against him should he be sued on the old note by any holder of it in due course. Many persons have suffered by their carelessness or ignorance in supposing that the substitution of the new note for the old frees them completely from liability on the latter one

TRUSTS AND TRUSTEES.

A trust arises when property of any kind is held by a person called the trustee for the benefit of another person or other persons called the beneficiaries or *cestuis-que-trust*. A trustee may hold property for the benefit of himself in conjunction with others. Any act or neglect of the trustee not allowed or excused by the instrument creating the trust or by law is called a breach of trust.

A corporation may act as a trustee. There may be one or more trustees of the same property, and the cestuis-que-trust also may be one or several.

Private trusts are those in which the trustees hold the property on behalf of individuals; public trusts those in which they hold it for charities or public purposes. Only the former will be dealt with here.

An express trust arises where the property is placed in the hands of the trustee for the express purpose of his using or managing it for the benefit of others. Such trusts are usually created by wills, marriage settlements, and trust deeds of certain other kinds.

An implied or constructive trust arises when the law provides or the circumstances of the case make it clear that property of any kind is held by one person not for his own benefit, or for his own benefit solely, but for that of other people. A mortgagee, for instance, who has sold the land of a mortgagor in default becomes a trustee for the mortgagor in respect of any money received in excess of the amount required to pay the mortgage debt and charges.

An executor or administrator also, though not expressly appointed a trustee, holds the property of the deceased on trust for those beneficially interested in it.

The powers and duties of a trustee are regulated by the will, settlement, or other writing appointing him, in so far as it clearly lays them down; but there are also many general rules defining them in default of any express mention in the writing creating the trust.

Acceptance of a trust is sometimes declared by the trustee in writing, but more generally is to be gathered by his exercise of some of the powers which the trust confers on him.

POWERS OF TRUSTEES—Generally speaking, the powers of trustees include everything necessary to allow of them managing and preserving the property committed to their charge in the most efficient way for the benefit of those interested in it. They act as owners, except that they do not apply any of the trust property or its proceeds to their own use.

Usually the method of appointment of new trustees is provided for in the deed creating the trust. In the absence of any provision to the contrary, a sole trustee who has accepted a trust, and becomes unwilling to act on it, has the power to appoint a new trustee in his place. If there are two or more trustees, and one dies or retires, the others may exercise this power.

A trustee must act himself, since confidence is reposed in him personally, and cannot delegate his powers to another except in case of necessity, or where authorised by the court, while he holds the office; but he may employ agents, such as solicitors, bankers, auctioneers, and rent collectors. He will be personally responsible only for due care in choosing these agents, and not for their fraud or default.

Trustees may bring all actions and settle all claims according to their best judgment in administering the trust. All of them, when there are more than one, must join in doing so, and receipts of capital must be signed by all of them, unless the settlement authorises one of them to give good receipts and discharges. As a general rule, it is permissible to allow one to receive income, such as rents. In some cases, also, from necessity, a co-trustee may be permitted to receive moneys. Where not otherwise directed by the instrument creating the trust, or unless some particular mode of investment is there prescribed, trustees in Victoria are empowered to invest the trust funds in— (1) First mortgage of lands, lending not more than 3/5 of the value put upon them by a competent valuer. (2) In Government debentures or other Government securities; in Treasury bonds; in debentures of the Melbourne and Metropolitan Board of Works or of the Melbourne Harbour Trust; in debentures issued by any city, town, shire, or borough in Victoria; and in numerous other securities authorised by various Acts of Parliament.

In other States special investments are authorised by statute; but in all of them and in England investment on first mortgage is permitted.

Where land is given to one person on trust for another, the trustee has, as a general rule, no power to sell, unless it is expressly or impliedly given to him by the instrument creating the trust.

ADVICE FROM THE COURT—In all cases of difficulty in understanding what is his duty, or in carrying it out, the trustee is empowered to apply to the Supreme Court for directions, and the costs of so doing will be allowed out of the trust property. The trustee may apply upon a written statement to a judge of the Supreme Court for advice in any particular matter, and in acting upon such advice he will be exonerated from any liability. But in this proceeding he makes the statements upon which the court advises him upon his own responsibility, and if they are erroneous he would not be excused if he should act detrimentally to the trust estate in consequence of the advice given upon the erroneous statement of facts. Where there are conflicting interests, or where the matter is complicated, the trustee should proceed by what is known as Originating Summons, bringing before the court all the persons interested in the matter, or at least giving them notice of the application, so that they may, if they choose, appear at court and look after their interests.

When a trustee holds property in trust for an infant (a person under the age of 21 years) he is allowed to apply as much as may be required of the income of the property for the infant's maintenance, education, and benefit, paying the money to the infant's parent or guardian for that purpose, or otherwise applying it at his discretion.

When the value of the property held by the trustee for an infant or person attaining a specified age does not exceed £2000, and when the income is insufficient to provide for the infant's maintenance and education, the trustee may apply to a judge in chambers, who is empowered to order the sale of the whole or any portion of the property, and to direct investment of the proceeds. If the income is still insufficient to maintain and educate the infant, the judge may direct the use of as much of the principal as may be necessary for that purpose.

REMUNERATION OF TRUSTEES — The theory of the law is that a trustee cannot charge for his time and trouble except where he has expressly stipulated for remuneration or it is allowed by the instrument creating the trust. But in Victoria and other States of Australia the court is empowered to allow commission to the trustee of deceased person's estates. It may do this even though the will provides for the trustee's commission, if it should consider such provision inadequate. Usually the remuneration is provided for in the will or deed creating the trust. It is also customary to provide that, where the trustee is a solicitor, he may charge for professional services, otherwise he, or a firm of which he is a member, would not be allowed to do so. A trustee may charge the property with all expenses out of pocket, and with the cost of paying all proper agents employed by him in administering the trust.

The remuneration of trustee companies, which are incorporated solely for the purpose of carrying on the business of executors and trustees, is authorised by the various Acts under which they are constituted. By their acts they are empowered to charge at a rate not exceeding $2\frac{1}{2}$ per cent. upon capital and 5 per cent. on income. Each company, as a rule, has a published rate of charges, beyond which it is not authorised to ask further payment. Special arrangements, of course, may be made by agreement.

REMOVAL OF TRUSTEES—Trustees may be removed by the court for misconduct in administering the trust. The persons to bring action against them are the beneficiaries, or one of them, and in the case of an infant the action is brought in his name by his next friend.

Misconduct includes gross negligence, disregard of the provisions of the trust, and any form of fraud on the beneficiaries. Trustees are bound to present accounts of their administration when ordered to do so by the court, and whether removed from the position of trustee or not, they must refund to the estate any loss suffered by their misconduct.

CONCLUSION OF A TRUST—Trustees are sometimes appointed for a specified term of years, or until the happening of a certain event, such as the coming of age or the marriage of the youngest of those interested in the estate. In this case, at the proper time, the trustee hands over the property to the person entitled, and the trust is at an end.

It sometimes happens that a will or other instrument gives property to trustees to hold for the benefit of persons who are all of full age, and imposes on the trustees restrictions against the sale or division of the property. In such a case, if all the persons interested in the property agree in requesting the trustee to disregard any of the provisions of the trust, he will be safe in doing so on receiving an indemnity from them. He may, in fact, put an end to the trust, and make any disposal of the property which he is requested to do.

Before doing this, however, he must be very certain that all possible claimants to the property, or any part of it, concur in the request, and that none of them is under any disability which prevents a valid assent to the trustee's action. It is not the duty of the trustee to run the slightest risk of future claims being brought against him in order to oblige the beneficiaries; but if there is no doubt that such persons have the sole beneficial interest in the property, he is bound to give effect to their wishes.

STATUTES OF LIMITATIONS.

These have been introduced from time to time for the reason that public welfare demands that the assertion of any right against another in a court of law should be made within a reasonable time, when the matter is fresh, and it is still open to either party to procure satisfactory proofs. Accordingly, where a person has "slept upon his rights," he will be prevented from reopening stale demands, the evidence to rebut which may not at that time be available.

The Statute 21, James I., c. 16, which is still in force in Australia, first dealt with the matter; and numerous English and Australian Acts contain provisions as to the time within which an action must be brought in respect of particular matters.

Generally, actions on any simple contract (i.e., not under seal) must be brought within six years from the time when the right to bring an action first arose; but an acknowledgment *in writing*—a verbal acknowledgment is not sufficient—of any debt will revive the right of action from the time of such acknowledgment, even after the six years, and the period of six years will once more begin to run from the date of such acknowledgment. A debt by specialty (i.e., under seal) is barred after fifteen years, but may be revived by an acknowledgment in writing, or part payment of any principal or interest due on the specialty debt. No distress can be made nor action to recover land brought after fifteen years from the accrual of the right to make the distress or entry on the land.

Actions for all common law wrongs must be brought also within 6 years, except an action for slander, which must be brought within two, or for injuries to the person, which must be within four, years after the act complained of. Where the defendant is beyond the seas at the time of the right of action arising, the time runs against the plaintiff only from his return. As against a person under disability, such as an infant, the statute of limitations does not begin to run until the removal of the disability: A disability arising after the period of limitation has begun will not prevent the operation of the statute; nor will the fact that a party did not know a right of action existed. So, if the cause of action were complete in a person's lifetime, the statute would begin and continue from that time, and not from his death, or the time of obtaining probate.

COPYRIGHT.

Copyright is the exclusive privilege of authorising the printing, selling, publishing, or delivering literary, musical, or artistic work. It was doubtful how far such a right was given by the common law ; but the statute 8 Anne c., 19, first conferred the privilege for a term of fourteen years. Each State has its Copyright Acts and English statutes in force. By Section 51 of the Commonwealth Constitution Act, the Federal Parliament is given power to make laws relating to copyright. This power has been carried out by the Copyright Act 1905.

The copyright of a book, dramatic or musical work, and the lecturing right in a lecture, subsist for the term of forty-two years, or for the author's life and seven years, whichever shall be the longer. If the work is posthumous, the copyright will endure for forty-two years from publication.

WILLS.

A will is a document executed in a certain prescribed form, which takes effect after the death of
the maker, to dispose of property and to exercise
various other powers.

The maker of a will is called a testator. An addition to a will is called a codicil; persons appointed
by a will to carry out its provisions are called executors.

No person under the age of twenty-one years is
capable of making a valid will.

Everything which a testator possesses, and which
he is capable of transferring to any other person,
may be disposed of by will. Property acquired after
the making of the will, and rights to property, on the
happening of events which may not occur until after
the death of the testator, as well as property possessed by him at the time of making the will, may be
so disposed of.

The will speaks as from the death of the testator,
and operates on every transmissible property or right
which he then possesses and which the will deals
with.

Examples of future rights to property are found
in marriage settlements, which frequently provide
that property shall be enjoyed by the parties to the
marriage for their lives, and go afterwards to children
who may be born of the marriage. Though such a
child die during its parents' lifetime, the settlement
may give it a right to dispose by will of the property
which would have come to it on the death of its

parents in the event of its outliving them. Such a future interest in property is called a "vested interest."

CONDITIONS OF VALIDITY—In order that a will may be valid it must comply with the following conditions:—

(1) It must be in writing, and signed by the testator, or by some other person in his presence and at his direction. (2) The signature must be made or acknowledged by the testator in the presence of two or more witnesses, both present at the same time. (3) The witnesses must subscribe their names as witnesses of the testator's signature, but they need not describe themselves as such in any particular form of words.

Nevertheless, in order to avoid doubts or trouble and expense when probate of the will is asked for, it is advisable to use the "attestation clause"—that is, the clause declaring that the will has been properly signed and witnessed, which is used in the form of will hereunder.

Where a person is, from illiteracy or illness, unable to write, he should affix his mark by making a cross in place of signature.

Form of will giving everything to one person.

This is the last Will and Testament of me [Christian name and surname], of [place of residence and occupation or calling]. I give, devise, and bequeath all my real and personal property of every description to [name and description of person] absolutely. And I appoint the said [name of person] sole executor [or executrix] of this my Will, and revoke all Wills by me at any time heretofore made, and declare this writing to be my last Will and Testament. In witness whereof I hereunto set my hand this —— day

of —— in the year of our Lord One thousand
nine hundred and ——.

Signature of Testator.

Signed by the said
[name of testator]
in the presence of
us, who, at his re-
quest, and in his
presence and in the
presence of each
other, at the same
time, have sub-
scribed our names
as witnesses.

Signatures of witnesses,
with their addresses
and occupations.

If the testator is unable to write, the following
words must be added to the attestation clause after
the word testament, namely, " the contents having
been first read over and explained to him."

It is inadvisable to use any figures or abbreviations
in a will. Everything should be written out at full
length.

WITNESSES—The witnesses to a will need not
be persons of full age provided they are old enough
to understand the nature of the act they are doing.

They must sign their names after, and not before,
the testator has done so.

If there are any interlineations, erasures, or correc-
tions in any part of the will or codicil, they must be
initialled by the testator and the witnesses in the
margin opposite to them. This should be done
before the will itself is signed. No alterations or
additions to it whatever should be made after signing,
except in the form of a properly-executed codicil.

No person who receives any benefit under a will,
nor the husband or wife of such a person, should be
a witness to it, because any gift by will to a witness,
or the husband or wife of a witness, is absolutely void.
The validity of the will is not affected by the witness
being a person whom the will purports to benefit.
All gifts or dispositions made by it are good except
those to the witness or the witness's husband or wife.
But a person who is benefited by a will may witness
a codicil without risk, and similarly a person benefited
by a codicil may witness the will.

REVOCATION—A will may be revoked or cancelled in various ways.

(1) By the marriage of the testator. (2) By tear-
ing off the signature, or by burning or otherwise
destroying the will. To act as a revocation, this must
be done by the testator hmself or by some person
at his request. If done by an unauthorised person,
it does not destroy the effect of the will, if evidence
is available as to its provisions. (3) By a subsequent
will, or a writing similarly signed and witnessed, and
declaring an intention to revoke. (4) By a codicil
which is considered part of the will, and may revoke
any part of it.

A revoked will can be revived only by a writing
signed and witnessed in the same manner as a will.

CONSTRUCTION   OF   WILLS — Technical
words are not necessary in a will, but if technical
words are used, they will be construed in their technical sense, unless there is a clear indication bv the
testator that they are not so used.

The court will always endeavour to give effect to
the testator's intention ; but if he uses technical words,
and leaves property to which thev aptly apply, it will
be assumed that his intention was to restrict them to
such property. Thus the word "devise" applies ·
primarily to real estate, and "bequeath" to person-

alty. Testators frequently use these terms indiscriminately, and the court is often called upon to decide whether by a " devise " of all his property a testator intends to distribute everything he possessed, or only his lands. The words ordinarily used to cover a gift of everything are, " I give, devise, and bequeath."

Unskilled testators are strongly advised to get professional assistance always, where practicable, in making a will, to be sure that their real intentions are effectively carried out.

Every will is construed as though it were executed immediately previous to the death of the testator, and is not affected by any changes in his affairs between the dates of making the will and of his death, in so far as it is possible to carry out its provisions.

Where certain portions of a testator's property are given to certain persons, and the residue is given to others, everything not specifically mentioned goes into the residue, and is taken by the person entitled to it. If certain portions of the property are specifically disposed of, and there is no gift of the residue to any person, the testator is deemed to be intestate as regards it, and it is distributed among those persons who would have taken it had he made no will.

Where from any reason it is impossible to give effect to any specific gift in the will the property comprised in it goes into the residue.

The word child or children in a will means legitimate children, unless there is a very clear indication to the contrary. Therefore, where it is desired to provide for an illegitimate child, great care should be taken to make the intention unmistakable by naming or otherwise clearly describing it.

REASONS FOR UPSETTING WILLS—A will may be set aside if it is proved that the testator was of unsound mind, or that he was persuaded to execute the will by fraud, or that he was of weak mind, and subjected to undue influence.

What constitutes mental unsoundness in the testator, or undue influence on the part of others sufficient to invalidate a will, is matter for decision in each case where the question is raised. Suspicion is usually felt of a will conferring large benefits upon persons by whom, or by whose agent, it was prepared, or of a will in favour of any person such as a doctor, minister, or confidential adviser, who may have been in constant touch with the testator when the will was executed, especially if he was then at the point of death, or in weak health.

Mental unsoundness sufficient to invalidate a will is not established by mere eccentricity, or even by certain insane delusions, unless the testator's mind appears to have been affected in such a way as to influence him in the disposition of his property. If he had in fact the " disposing mind "—that is, if he thoroughly understood and intended what he has done, the will is valid, although the testator may have disregarded moral obligations in distributing his estate.

In the event of a will being set aside, the testator's property is disposed of as though he had died intestate.

Glossary of Legal Terms Commonly Met With.

ABUSE OF PROCESS.—When a litigant endeavours to use the procedure of the courts to obtain some unwarranted advantage over his opponent, generally by putting him to useless expense. The court will strike out any proceeding which is an abuse of its process.

ACCESSORY.—One who is not a chief actor at a felony, but connected before or afterwards with it. If he procures the committing of a felony, he is an accessory before the fact; if, knowing a felony has been committed, he assists the felon, he is an accessory after the fact.

ACCORD AND SATISFACTION.—When one person has a right of action against another, an agreement is sometimes made that the latter should do, and the former accept, something else in discharge thereof. There must be consideration. For example, the payment of £10 would not be an answer to a debt of £50; but if any additional benefit to the debtor be thrown in, that will be sufficient to turn the scale, and make it binding. The taking of a negotiable instrument would be a good satisfaction for a debt of greater amount, if given and taken on that understanding, since the fact of negotiability makes it a different thing. When an agreement of this nature has been made and carried out, it is called *accord and satisfaction,* and is a complete answer to the original claim.

ACT OF GOD.—An act of God, in the contemplation of the law, means such a direct, violent, sudden, and irresistible act of nature as could not by any amount of ability have been foreseen; or, if foreseen, could not by any amount of human care and skill have been resisted. It is usual in contracts to except any liability for non-performance arising from an "act of God;" the events excepted would then comprise all natural accidents which it is practically impossible to foresee or guard against, as an extraordinary storm, an earthquake, an exceptional fall of rain or snow. To be included under the term "act of God," the accident must not be attributable to the agency of man. When any duty is imposed by the law itself, there is always an implied exception of the act of God. For example, a carrier is, by the common law, answerable for damage to goods carried by him; but if he can show that by no reasonable precaution could the loss have been prevented, the misadventure amounts to an "act of God," and he is not liable.

When the duty arises under a contract, however, its performance is not generally excused unless an act of God is expressly mentioned in the contract, or unless it is evident that this was clearly contemplated by the parties as affording an excuse for a breach of the contract.

ADVERSE POSSESSION.—Occupation of land by some person who holds adversely to—that is, without any authority from the real owner. After such continuous occupation for fifteen years the owner's claim to possession is barred, and the unauthorised occupier acquires a title by adverse possession. Land unoccupied is deemed to be in the possession of the real owner; so that if an unauthorised occupier remained in possession for ten years, and then went away for a year, and subsequently returned, his adverse possession would commence again only from the date of his second occupation. The real owner would not be displaced until the expiry of fifteen years from the latter date.

AFFILIATION.—The fixing of the paternity of, and obligation to maintain, an illegitimate child. By the Act, No. 1684, in Victoria a woman who is enceinte may recover before two justices a sum not exceeding ten pounds for pre-maternity or confinement expenses upon proof of her condition, and that the person summoned is responsible for it. An order for pre-maternity expenses will not be made on the uncorroborated oath of the woman without some other evidence. The order will lapse if no child be born within five months. Payment under any order is made to the clerk of petty sessions, who keeps the amounts paid until the birth of a living or still-born child, when it is applied in accordance with the order. If no confinement takes place at the expiration of five months, the moneys paid are handed back to the person against whom the order was made. "Confinement expenses," under the Act, mean reasonable medical and nursing expenses, and clothing for the child.

AFFIDAVIT.—A written statement sworn before some person authorised to receive oaths. Evidence in court is usually given *viva-voce*—that is, by ordinary spoken testimony; but in some matters it is given on affidavit.

ALIBI means " elsewhere." An accused person frequently sets up the defence that he was not at the place where the crime was committed. If he succeeds in doing so, he " proves an alibi."

ANCIENT LIGHT.—A defined aperture in a building through which light has been obtained continuously for twenty years. The owner, unless the access of light during this time has been obtained by agreement, then acquires a right to light, and can prevent his neighbour from obstructing it. Unless the right had actually been acquired before the 8th October, 1907, no right of light can be thus acquired in Victoria.

ARSON.—The malicious setting-on-fire of a house or other building.

ASSAULT.—An actual attempt to interfere physically with another, as by touching or striking. Words do not constitute an assault.

ASSIGN.—(1) To transfer property; to set over a right to another. (2) The person appointed by another to do any act, or who takes some right from another who is called the assignor.

ASSOCIATE.—The name given to an officer who acts as private secretary to a judge of the Supreme Court, and arranges routine matters before that judge.

ATTACHMENT.—A process by which, at the discretion of a judge, a person who is guilty of some contempt of court, by neglecting to obey some order or otherwise, is brought up for punishment.

ATTORNMENT.—In order to better secure the interest payable on a mortgage, the mortgagor frequently " attorns," or becomes tenant to the mortgagee. This gives the mortgagee a right of distress.

ATTORNEY.—(1) Originally a person authorised to issue process in the courts of common law. A solicitor acted similarly in the courts of Chancery; a proctor in the Ecclesiastical and Admiralty Courts. The term " solicitor " is now generally employed to, cover the functions of all three. (2) One appointed to do something in the absence, or to act in the place of, the person appointing him. The document by which he is so appointed is called a " Power of Attorney."

AUTREFOIS CONVICT.—A plea in criminal cases. When a person has been once convicted, he cannot afterwards be proceeded against for the same offence. The rule of law is that no one shall be twice harassed for the same offence.

AUTREFOIS ACQUIT.—A plea in criminal cases. When a person has been formerly acquitted, he cannot afterwards be proceeded against for the same offence.

BAIL.—To set at liberty a person arrested or imprisoned on security being taken for his appearance when called up for trial.

The money guaranteed or paid for this purpose is also called Bail.

BAILMENT.—The delivery of a thing in trust for some special object or purpose. The person delivering is called the bailor; the person receiving the bailee. Thus a pawnbroker who receives jewels or plate as a security for payment receives them as a bailee in trust to hold and deliver them up on repayment. A carrier is the bailee of goods entrusted to him to deliver.

BATTERY.—An intentional beating or wounding. It always includes an assault; but an assault may not amount to a battery.

BEQUEST.—A gift of personal property in a will.

BETTING.—Bets are not recoverable at law; and the carrying on of betting is prohibited by various enactments.

BIGAMY.—The offence of a husband or wife marrying again during the life of the other. It is a felony. When either husband or wife has not been heard of for seven years, there is a presumption of law that he or she is dead. If either party then re-married, he or she would not be guilty of bigamy; but the second marriage would be void if the other party were still living.

BOND.—A written acknowledgment under seal of a debt or obligation to do something. The person giving it is called the obligor; the person in whose favour it is given is known as the obligee.

BRIBERY.—The corrupt bestowal of some gift or favour upon any person in a public office or position of trust with the object of influencing him in the discharge of his duty.

BROKER.—An agent employed to make contracts in trade for a payment called brokerage.

BURGLARY.—A breaking or entering by night into a dwelling-house with the intention of committing a felony.

BY-LAW.—The laws or regulations of corporations and public bodies (such as shire or borough councils) for the government of their affairs. They are binding unless contrary to law.

CAPIAS means, literally, that " you may take." There are various writs of capias; but the word most frequently is used to denote the writ of capias in the form in the 8th schedule to the *Supreme Court Act 1890*, which may be granted when the plaintiff in any action in the Supreme Court satisfies a judge that he has a cause of action to the amount of twenty pounds, and that the defendant is about to leave Victoria, and the action will be thereby defeated. If a writ of capias is granted, the person against whom it is directed may be arrested within one month, and must remain in custody until he has given a bail-bond to the sheriff, or deposited the sum endorsed on the writ, with ten pounds for costs. Any person arrested can apply at once to any judge of the Supreme Court for an order that the plaintiff show cause why he should not be discharged; and the judge, after hearing the matter argued, makes such order as he thinks fit.

A writ of capias may be executed on a Sunday.

CAVEAT.—The Latin word "that he may beware." A process for stopping certain legal proceedings; for example, the granting of probate of a will. Any person who seeks to prevent such probate being granted may lodge a Caveat, a document warning the court not to do anything further without giving notice to him or her. The person lodging such notice is known as the Caveator or Caveatrix. The matter is then fought out on its merits.

CERTIORARI.—A Latin word, " to be more fully informed about." A writ of the Supreme Court, issued to inferior courts to remove the proceedings into the Supreme Court, to be there quashed or confirmed as that court may see fit.

CHAMPERTY.—An unlawful bargain between one of the parties to an action and a third person who has no interest in it, whereby the latter carries on the suit at his own expense in consideration of receiving the proceeds.

CODICIL.—A supplementary will, containing anything a testator wishes to add to or alter in the original will. It must be executed in the same manner as a will.

COLLUSION.—An agreement between two or more persons to do some act with an unlawful intention. In divorce proceedings, for example, an agreement between the petitioner and respondent, that the latter would not appear and oppose the granting of a decree *nisi*, would be collusion. [See *Divorce*.]

COMMITTEE of a lunatic—the person to whose care or custody a lunatic is committed.

COMMON LAW, as contrasted with statute law, receives its binding power from usage and universal acceptance. It is made up of a body of principles, which, by adoption, have become recognised as constituting part of the law of the country, and which are enforced by the courts. Where a statute abrogates or interferes with some principle of common law, the statute prevails and overrides that particular provision or usage of the common law.

COMPOUNDING A FELONY.—The taking back of stolen goods, or receiving other consideration, on an agreement not to prosecute the felon.

CONSIDERATION.—The inducement given to enter into a contract. It is essential to the validity of all contracts not under seal, and has been judicially defined as " some right, interest, profit, or benefit accruing to one party, or some forbearance, loss, or responsibility given, suffered, or undertaken by the other."

CONSPIRACY.—A combination or agreement between several persons to carry into effect some unlawful purpose.

CONTRIBUTORY.—A person liable to contribute to the extent of the amount not paid up upon his shares in the event of a company being wound up.

CONTRIBUTORY NEGLIGENCE is the failure to prevent the consequences arising from someone else's negligence, when this could have been done. Where a defendant who is sued alleges that the plaintiff was guilty of contributory negligence, he must show that the plaintiff might have avoided the consequences of his own negligence by the exercise of ordinary care; or that he could not have avoided the consequences of the plaintiff's negligence by the exercise of ordinary care.

COSTS BETWEEN PARTY AND PARTY — COSTS BETWEEN SOLICITOR AND CLIENT.—When costs are awarded by the court in any action or matter, unless the amount is fixed by the judge, they are ordered to be taxed. An officer of the court called the taxing officer then assesses what the unsuccessful party is to pay; the successful party brings in his "bill of costs," which includes all the items he claims, and the taxing officer "taxes off" or disallows those items which he considers should not be allowed. The usual order for costs allows costs to be recovered only as between party and party; in the case of trustees, however, and in other instances, where some special reason exists for the order, the court awards costs "as between solicitor and client." The effect of this is that practically every item of expenditure, unless it is quite unreasonable, is allowed to be charged by the successful party.

COVERTURE.—The condition of a woman during marriage, when she is under the cover or protection of her husband.

COVIN.—A secret agreement between two or more persons to injure another.

CRIME is defined in *Stephen's Commentaries* as "the violation of a right, when considered in reference to the evil tendency of such violation as regards the community at large."

CROSS-EXAMINATION.—The examination of a witness by his opponent, or his opponent's counsel. This is done after the examination-in-chief, which is the examination of a witness by or on behalf of the party by whom he is called as a witness.

DEED-POLL.—A deed executed by one person, setting forth the act and intention of the person executing it.

DEFEASANCE.—A deed which accompanies another, and declares that, upon the fulfilment of certain conditions, the other deed shall be of no effect.

DE FACTO.—In fact.

DE JURE.—Of right.

DEL CREDERE.—A factor who sells goods on credit for an extra consideration, called a del credere commission, guarantees that the purchaser is solvent and will complete the purchase.

DEVISE.—A gift of real estate or land in a will.

DUCES TECUM SUBPOENA.—Where a person has a document in his possession, he is served with this subpoena, commanding him to "bring with him" (duces tecum) the document to the trial.

EASEMENT.—A privilege which the owner of one landed property has over the property of another; for example, a right of way, or the right to receive light. The property to which the right is attached is known as the "dominant tenement;" that over which it is exercised is called the "servient tenement."

EJECTMENT.—An action to recover the possession of land and damages for wrongfully holding, or over-holding, it after the expiry of a lawful occupation.

EMBEZZLEMENT.—The unlawful appropriation to his own use by a servant or clerk of money or chattels received by him for or on account of his master or employer.

ESCROW.—A writing under seal delivered to A, to be given to B, as soon as some condition is fulfilled. Until the time of delivery it has no legal effect ; but so soon as the condition is fulfilled, and the delivery made, it ceases to be in "escrow," and becomes a binding deed.

ESTATE TAIL.—This was also a freehold estate of inheritance, but it was less than fee simple, being limited to a person and the heirs of his body; so that, except by certain methods, it could not be transferred out of the family to which it was granted. This tenure has never been of great importance in Australia, but is very common in England. In Victoria, since 1885, any words which formerly would have granted an estate tail confer an estate in fee simple.

EQUITY was originally the supplemental law administered in the chancellor's courts to assist the defects of the common law. It gave relief that could not be obtained in the ordinary courts of common law, on the principles of "equity and good conscience," compelling a defendant to do, or abstain from doing, any particular act. The distinction between equity and common law, which is historical, is now of no practical concern, as law and equity are administered in the same court, and where there is any conflict, the rules of equity prevail.

EXECUTION.—The last stage of an action by which possession is obtained of something recovered by a judgment, either specific property or money. [See "Fieri Facias."]

EXPARTE.—A proceeding by one party in the absence of the other.

FACTOR.—An agent employed to sell merchandise delivered to him for a commission. He differs from a broker in that he may sell in his own name, and has possession of, and a special property in, the goods.

FLAGRANTE DELICTO.—"In the act of committing a crime."

FORGERY.—The false alteration or making of an instrument with intent to defraud. The most common instance is where a person wrongfully imitates the signature of another to some document.

FELONY—MISDEMEANOUR.—Felony was originally a criminal offence, for which the estate of the culprit was forfeited in addition to the punishment awarded for the crime. It was distinguished from Misdemeanour, upon which no forfeiture followed. Nowadays this distinction is abolished, and felonies and misdemeanours are usually catalogued as such in various statutes. Misdemeanour is a crime less than felony; for example, murder is a felony, perjury is a misdemeanour. The punishments are regulated according to the gravity of the offence.

FIERI FACIAS.—Usually abbreviated to *Fi. Fa.;* literally "that you cause to be made." A judicial writ containing a command to the sheriff that he cause to be made of the goods and chattels of the party named therein the sum specified. It is a common mode of enforcing a judgment recovered in an action, as if the amount is not paid, the goods and chattels are sold by the sheriff.

FREEHOLD is the modern descendant of the old feudal tenure of land, known as "free socage." The services which the tenant rendered to the lord from whom he held were honourable, such as military services, and when feudalism ceased to exist the land was held free of any burden.

FEME SOLE.—An unmarried woman or widow.

FEME COUVERT.—A married woman.

FEE SIMPLE.—A freehold estate of inheritance with no qualifications. The possessor of the fee simple is the absolute owner, and can dispose of it as he will. The owner of a life estate in land, on the other hand, has only an interest terminating with his own life.

GARNISHEE.—Where A owes money to B, and B to C, and C recovers judgment against B, C may notify A, by the proper procedure, to pay him instead of B. A is called the Garnishee.

HABEAS CORPUS.—"That you may have the body." There are several writs of *Habeas Corpus*, but it is usually applied to the writ under the Statute 31, Car. II., c. 2. It commands anyone who is alleged to be detaining another in custody to produce the latter in court at the time named, and submit to the order of the Court. This writ is one of the "bulwarks of British liberty."

HEREDITAMENT.—Every kind of property that can be inherited. Anything in England that might descend to the heir was called a hereditament. The expression, "Lands, tenements, and hereditaments," was, and still is, used in legal documents to describe property in land, as distinguished from goods and chattels.

HOMICIDE.—The destroying of the life of a human being. Justifiable homicide is where no guilt attaches to the slayer; as where an officer kills someone who is resisting arrest; or where someone kills in self-defence another who has unlawfully attacked him.

IDEM SONANS.—"Of the like sound." Where a name in a writ or other legal proceeding is mis-spelt, but the sound is substantially the same, this will not inavlidate the proceedings, provided that the error is trifling. The Court will consider in each case whether the variation is sufficient to mislead.

INDICTMENT.—A proceeding whereby certain indictable offences are brought before a grand jury, summoned by the sheriff in obedience to an order of the Full Court. The strict legal definition of an indictment is a written accusation of one or more persons of a crime preferred to, and presented on oath, by a grand jury.

INDICTABLE OFFENCE.—All treasons, felonies, and misdemeanours, whether created by statute or existing at common law, are indictable offences.

IN COURT—IN CHAMBERS.—Certain matters can be decided by a judge without the formalities and procedure prescribed for applications to the court. These are heard "in chambers," and it is not necessary for counsel to appear. In court applications can only be made by barristers or solicitors, who are expected to wear wig and gown, or the parties in person.

INFORMATION AND COMPLAINT.—An information is usually applied to the mode of initiating proceedings before justices in criminal matters or offences punishable by penalties. It is the preliminary statement of the complainant's case upon which the justice issues his summons, or, if he think fit, when the information is on oath, his warrant. In civil matters the preliminary statement of the plaintiff's claim, upon which a justice issues his summons to the defendant to appear and dispute it if he wish to do so, is called a complaint.

IN FORMA PAUPERIS.—Where a person is not worth £25, in addition to his wearing apparel, and lays facts before counsel, who certifies that on those facts he has a good case, he is allowed to proceed without payment of the ordinary court fees for process.

INFANT.—Any person, male or female, under the age of 21 years.

INHERITANCE.—A perpetual or continuing right to an estate. It is often contrasted with the word "purchase," an estate by purchase being one acquired otherwise than by descent or inheritance.

INJUNCTION.—An order of the court, by which a person is required to abstain from doing a specified act. An "interlocutory" injunction is one made until the trial of an action, in order to preserve the property concerning which the dispute has arisen in the same condition until the merits of the dispute are decided. A "perpetual" injunction is one that prohibits the act for all time, and is made at the trial of the action.

INTERLOCUTORY PROCEEDING.—Some proceeding in an action other than the final hearing. It includes various applications that may be necessary as to pleadings, discovery, summonses.

INTERPLEADER.—Where one has moneys or property not his own, in respect of which he expects to be sued by two or more parties claiming adversely, he may obtain relief by bringing them and the property before the court, and leaving them to fight out the question of ownership.

INTERROGATORY.—A question in writing put by one party to another in an action in the Supreme or County Courts before trial, which, if relevant, the party interrogated must answer upon oath. Interrogatories are used as a means of facilitating proof, and binding the opponent down to definite statements, so that evidence may be procured to meet his case. Leave must be obtained from a judge before interrogatories can be administered, as they frequently increase the expenses of an action.

LACHES.—A legal term for negligence or omission of duty.

LARCENY.—The wilfully wrongful or fraudulent taking possession of the goods of another with a felonious intent to deprive the owner of his property in them. In Victoria and most of the States the definition of larceny has been extended to cover the failing to account for property which has been received by anyone as the clerk or agent of another, even although it was not his duty to hand over the identical property in the state in which he received it.

LEADING QUESTION.—A question put to a witness which suggests its own answer. Such questions are only allowed on cross-examination, except under special circumstances, because a witness is expected to tell his own story of what he did and observed.

LEX SCRIPTA.—The written or statute law, as distinguished from the common law.

LIEN.—A right to retain something belonging to another, of which a person has possession until certain claims of his are satisfied.

LIFE ASSURANCE COMPANIES AND TRUSTEE COMPANIES.—The law relating to these, so far as it affects the average citizen, will be found under "Life Assurance" and "Trusts."

LOCUS STANDI.—The right of a person to appear in a matter before the Court. Sometimes in equity suits, where there are numerous parties, the right of one or more to be heard upon any particular question may be disputed.

MALA IN SE.—Acts, such as murder, which are "wrong in themselves," as distinguished from *mala prohibita*, which are acts made unlawful by reason of the prohibition of some statute.

MANDAMUS.—A writ issued to enforce the performance of some public duty by a public officer where there is no other remedy. The court has a discretion to grant or refuse it. A Mandamus may also be claimed by, and granted to, the plaintiff in an action in order to enforce the performance of a duty.

MANSLAUGHTER.—The unlawful killing of another without malice, either express or implied. Express malice is the positive possession of an intention to cause death or bodily injury, which, in the ordinary course of nature, may cause death. Implied malice is the possession of a general intention implied from the acts of the offender; or the wanton running of a risk by a person who knows that the act he commits will probably cause death, or bodily injury that may result in death.

MESNE PROFITS.—The profits derived from land while the possession has been wrongfully withheld from the true owner, or used without his consent.

MESSUAGE.—A dwelling-house, with out-buildings and land used in connection with it.

MINER'S RIGHT.—A document issued by the Governor-in-Council to be in force for any number of years not exceeding fifteen. Anyone may obtain it for a fee of two shillings and sixpence for every year for which the right is to be in force. It is necessary to authorise the person to mine on Crown lands. Its possessor may peg out a " claim "—that is, a parcel of Crown land, of which he takes possession in accordance with the bye-laws of any mining board, and has various privileges of cutting timber, constructing dams and races, and diverting water, set out in the *Mines Acts.*

A " Consolidated Miner's Right " is issued on the application of the manager or trustee of a company of persons who have agreed to work any claims in partnership.

MURDER was long ago defined by Lord Coke thus— " When a person of sound memory and discretion unlawfully killeth any reasonable creature in being and under the King's peace with malice aforethought, either express or implied."

NISI PRIUS.—The term dates back to the reign of Edward I. Justices were appointed to hear cases in the different counties, and a trial would be ordered to take place at Westminster unless before (nisi prius) the date fixed it had taken place in the county. The term is now popularly used to denote the trial in the first place before a judge or judge and jury, as distinguished from its final adjudication on appeal.

NECESSARIES.—Goods suitable to the condition in life and the actual requirements of the purchaser at the time of the sale and delivery. An infant or person mentally incapacitated, to whom necessaries are sold and delivered, must pay a reasonable price for them. For goods other than necessaries an infant is not liable. What are necessaries must be decided as a fact in each case. Sir William Anson, in his "Law of Contract," instances a wild animal and steam-roller as two things which could hardly, under any circumstances, be deemed necessaries.

NEGLIGENCE in law has been defined by Baron Alderson as "the omission to do something which a reasonable man, guided upon those considerations which ordinarily regulate the conduct of human affairs, would do, or doing something which a prudent and reasonable man would not do." It is a ground of legal liability when the party whose conduct is in question is in a situation in which is imposed on him the duty of taking care.

NEXT FRIEND—GUARDIAN AD LITEM.—An infant brings an action by his next friend, who is some adult, other than a married woman. An infant defends an action or appears when served with any process by a guardian ad litem. A married woman cannot act in either capacity.

NOLLE PROSEQUI.—"To decline to prosecute." Although not strictly so confined, this phrase is generally understood to refer to the determination of the Crown, when satisfied before the hearing that the charge against an accused person cannot be proved, not to proceed further against him.

NULLA BONA.—A return made by the sheriff that there is no property to satisfy the writ, where he has been ordered to issue execution. [See Execution: Fieri Facias.]

ORDER NISI—ORDER ABSOLUTE.—An order *nisi* is a conditional order made by the court, e.g., in its divorce or insolvency jurisdiction. It is made absolute on the expiry of the time stated in the order *nisi*, unless (*nisi*) some reason is shown to the court why this should not be done. The order, when made absolute, is final.

ORIGINATING SUMMONS.—A special kind of summons most commonly adopted in the administration of estates where questions of difficulty arise, but where the facts are not in dispute. The parties are brought before the court at less expense than would be occasioned by a suit, and definite questions are put to the court, argued

PAROL.—Literally, "by word of mouth." As applied to agreements, it is also used in law to refer to any agreement not under seal, although in writing.

PERJURY.—The crime committed by any person who, when a lawful oath has been administered to him in a proceeding in a Court of Justice or before some competent tribunal, swears wilfully and falsely in a matter material to the issue or point in question.

PENDENTE LITE.—"During Litigation." In a divorce suit, for example, an order is made for payment of alimony to the wife *pendente lite* until the suit is concluded.

PLEADINGS.—The technical name for the formal statement in writing of the claim and defence in an action in the Supreme Court. They usually consist of a statement of claim by the plaintiff; a statement of defence by the defendant, who, if he has any claim against the plaintiff, may raise it by a counter-claim, and a reply on behalf of the plaintiff to the defence, and, where there is one, to the counter-claim. The pleadings are filed in court, and the parties cannot raise any issues not contained in them, unless they obtain leave from the court to amend. The object of the pleadings is that both parties may come to trial with a definitely stated case.

PRESENTMENT.—A proceeding by the Attorney or Solicitor-General, or a Crown Prosecutor, in the Supreme Court or Court of General Sessions, by which a person accused of any indictable offence is presented for trial.

PRESCRIPTION.—A title from long-continued possession. [See Adverse Possession].

PRIMA FACIE.—"At first appearance." *Prima facie evidence* is that which raises so strong an appearance of probability that it is accepted as sufficient proof, unless evidence to the contrary is given to refute or conradict it. *Conclusive evidence* is proof which is beyond the possibility of contradiction.

PROHIBITION.—A writ issued from the Supreme Court to an inferior court not to proceed with a cause, on the ground that it has no jurisdiction.

PUISNE.—A puisné judge is a title used to describe the judges of the Supreme Court other than the Chief Justice. It is derived from the French puis né "born after," and so "coming after" the Chief Justice.

QUASH.—To overthrow or make of no effect, as when a Superior Court, on appeal, quashes the order of the Court appealed from.

QUI TAM.—A "qui tam" action is one in which an informer is allowed to sue for, and recover, a penalty. *Qui tam pro domino rege quam pro se ipso sequitur*—"Who sues on behalf of our lord the king as well as on his own."

QUO WARRANTO.—A Crown writ directed against anyone claiming or usurping any public office or franchise, which requires him to show "by what authority" he supports his claim.

RECOGNISANCE.—The person bound by a recognisance acknowledges that he is indebted to the Crown in the sum specially ordered, with a condition that it shall be void if he appear in court on such a day. If he fails to do so, the recognisances are *estreated*—that is, the sum becomes payable.

REPLEVIN.—An action to recover possession of goods alleged to have been unlawfully taken; applied almost exclusively to the taking of goods in distress for rent. An action for damages for illegal distress is more usual.

Provision is made under the *Landlord and Tenant Act* for allowing the person distrained upon to "replevy" or take back the things seized on giving a bond for twice their value to prosecute the suit and return them if a return be ordered.

RESIDUE.—The surplus of a testator's estate after all debts have been paid. A residuary legatee is the person to whom has been left all that remains of the estate, after paying debts and legacies particularly given.

SALE OF GOODS.—A contract of sale of goods is defined by the *Sale of Goods Act 1896* to be a contract whereby the seller transfers or agrees to transfer the property in goods to the buyer for a money consideration called the price. Where the property passes at once, the contract is called a sale; but where the transfer of the property in the goods is to take place at a future time, or subject to some condition thereafter to be fulfilled, the contract is called an agreement to sell. An agreement to sell becomes a sale when the time elapses or the conditions are fulfilled. Traders should provide themselves with a copy of the Act No. 1422, where the law relating to the sale of goods is codified.

SUBPOENA.—Literally, "under a penalty." A writ requiring the attendance of the person on whom it is served in Court, under a penalty if he does not appear.

SUMMONS.—Every action in the Supreme Court is commenced by a writ of summons, but this is usually known as the writ.

The ordinary meaning of summons is a process by which one party brings the other before a judge to settle matters of detail in an action, or such other matters as are authorised by statute to be determined on summons. It is heard by a judge in chambers.

SUMMONS FOR DIRECTIONS.—An interlocutory proceeding in a Supreme Court action by which either party may require the other to attend before a judge, who then gives directions how the action is to proceed, and decides whether there will be pleadings, interrogatories, etc., where the trial is to take place, and whether with or without a jury.

TRESPASS.—" Any invasion of private property, be it ever so minute, is a trespass," was laid down in the famous case of *Entick v. Carrington*, the leading case in regard to the power to arrest and seize papers under a warrant issued by a Secretary of State. A personal injury is a trespass to the person. The popular notice that " Trespassers will be prosecuted " may be, as it generally is, disregarded. The trespasser is liable to a civil action for damages, but would not be liable to prosecution by the mere entry without any felonious intent.

TIPSTAFF.—A constable connected with the courts. In Australia tipstaffs are the somewhat superfluous orna-. ments of the High Court.

TENEMENT.—Literally, a thing held. In popular language it is applied to houses. [See " Hereditament."]

TROVER.—An action for recovering the value of goods which, it is alleged, another has wrongfully converted to his own use.

TORT.—A wrong or injury which gives rise to an action at the suit of the injured party for damages. A crime is an offence for which punishment is awarded by fine or imprisonment.

ULTRA VIRES—" beyond the powers;" usually applied to a company or local council doing some act, or passing some regulation or by-law, which it has no power to do, and which, therefore, is of no effect.

USUFRUCT.—The right of enjoying the fruits *(fructus)* of things belonging to others, without destroying the subject over which the right extends.

VENUE, originally meant the place from which a jury were to come for the trial. It is generally used to signify the place where an action or proceeding is to be tried.

VERDICT.—The determination of a jury declared to a judge. It may be a general verdict "for the plaintiff" or "for the defendant;" or a special verdict answering specific questions of fact left to the jury by the judge.

VESTED.—Estates may be vested in interest—that is, when there is a present right to future enjoyment; or vested in possession, where the right to enjoyment actually exists.

When the estate will only be enjoyed upon the happening of an event that may never happen, it is said to be *contingent;* for example, an estate to be given to a man if he attains 21.

WARRANT.—A precept to some officer of the law to arrest an offender, to be dealt with according to law.

WARRANTY.— A guarantee; also a promise or covenant by deed to warrant. In connection with the sale of goods, a warranty means an agreement with reference to goods, the breach of which does not give a right to repudiate the contract, but gives rise to a claim for damages. For instance, if the goods are found not to be up to a required standard, or unsuitable for the purpose for which they were obtained, the injured party may have a right to recover damages, though he could not set aside the contract. If it was a *condition* that the goods should be of a certain nature, failure to fulfil this condition would entitle the injured party to discharge the contract altogether. Whether an undertaking is a condition or a warranty is often a point of great nicety.

WITHOUT PREJUDICE.—When it is desired before or during the course of litigation to communicate with an opposing party, in order to effect a settlement of the dispute, such communication is frequently made "without prejudice." The effect of heading correspondence, or holding a verbal interview, "without prejudice" is that if the negotiations for settlement are unsuccessful, nothing that occurred in the correspondence or at the interview can be given in evidence unless both parties consent. For instance, A is suing B for £100; in order to save time and money, he may offer, without prejudice, to take £60. If this is refused, no evidence as to this offer could be given at the trial.

Fraser and Jenkinson, Printers, 345 Queen-street, Melbourne.

www.ingramcontent.com/pod-product-compliance
Lightning Source LLC
Chambersburg PA
CBHW021800190326
41518CB00007B/386